TASSAJARA
COOKBOOK

"When you cook,
you are not just working on food,
you are working on yourself,
you are working on others."

—SHUNRYU SUZUKI ROSHI

TASSAJARA COOKBOOK

lunches, picnics & appetizers

Karla Oliveira, M.S., R.D.

Photographs by

Patrick Tregenza and Renshin Judy Bunce

GIBBS SMITH
TO ENRICH AND INSPIRE HUMANKIND

First Edition
16 15 14 13 12   5 4 3 2 1

Text © 2007 Karla Oliveira, M.S., R.D.
Photographs © 2007 Patrick Tregenza and Renshin Judy Bunce

Published by
Gibbs Smith, Publisher
P.O. Box 667
Layton, Utah 84041

Orders: 1.800.835.4993
www.gibbs-smith.com

Designed by Black Eye Design
Printed and bound in China

Library of Congress Cataloging-in-Publication Dat
Oliveira, Karla.
Tassajara cookbook : lunches, picnics & appetizers / Karla Oliveira ; photographs by Patrick Tregenza and Renshin Judy Bunce. — 1st ed.
     p. cm.
 ISBN: 978-1-4236-0097-8 (hardcover)
 ISBN: 978-1-4236-3183-5 (paperback)
1. Vegetarian cookery. I. Title.

   TX837.O45 2007
   641.5'636—dc22

                     2007012378

*This book is dedicated
to my sons, Colin and Jackson,
for just being.*

contents

acknowledgments

I would like to thank David Zimmerman at Tassajara for his encouragement, valuable input, and being there to help with this book whenever needed.

To Sonja Gardenswartz for seeing her live her practice as Tenzo with patience and openness and for her faith in me to do this book.

To the Guest Cooks and Bag Lunch Crew past, present and future for their creativity over the years for making the Bag Lunch what it is today, and for bringing their kitchen practice into our lives. I would specifically like to acknowledge David, Anke, Mako, Kathy, Linda, Jana, Darcy, Raiwin, and the others who gave me input or left valuable notes on the Bag Lunch.

To Edward Espe Brown for his teachings, humor and generous spirit.

To my editor, Melissa Barlow, for her patience, insight and kindness. To Richard Raymond for his kind support over the years. And to my sons, Colin and Jackson, for their help in the kitchen and input with the recipes. And finally, to the San Francisco Zen Center for this wonderful opportunity.

I would also like to acknowledge some of the many cookbooks and sources used as the creative backbone for these recipes by the Guest Cooks. There are certainly more than I can list so please be assured, the Guest Cooks thank you. Some of the books are: *The Tassajara Recipe Book, Garden Feasts, Moosewood, The Tempeh Cookbook, Vegetarian Cooking for Everyone, The Unplugged Cookbook, Chez Panisse Desserts, World of the East, Vegetarian Appetizers,* and *The Garden of Vegan.*

foreword

What's for lunch? We all need to eat. And we have lunch in various ways: bag lunch, cafeteria, diner, burger place, deli or restaurant.

What's the occasion? Perhaps it's everyday on-the-go fueling up. Maybe it's just food, something to get done and out of the way, or maybe it's time for a break—a real respite and time for nourishment and sustenance.

During the Tassajara guest season, the Zen meditation community opens its gates to visitors, and since there's no radio, no TV, no movies, a few newspapers perhaps a day or two old, there is not much to do except eat.

Many of our visitors appreciate the chance to take a vacation and enjoy time being idle: napping, reading a book, having a cup of tea. Relaxing with a set menu, family-style breakfast and dinner, Tassajara guests are presented with a choice for lunch: "Would you care to eat in the dining room or make a bag lunch?"

Of course, if you haven't been to "Bag Lunch," you haven't a clue to the incredible extravagance—the luscious display of breads, cheeses, spreads, sauces, salsas, fruits, home-baked cookies, chips, guacamole, tomato slices, lettuces, nut butters, jams and jellies.

It's a far cry from the first bag lunches made forty years ago when the kitchen made them all the same: cheese sandwich, an apple or orange, some carrot or celery sticks, and a cookie. But this turned out to be down right frustrating for would-be flavor connoisseurs.

The solution was simple. Put out a display of ingredients and let people activate their innate capacity to make choices and improvise lunch. Now no two are the same!

We can give thanks to all those caring for and producing foods. And we can appreciate the hard work and generosity of time and spirit that Karla Oliveira has put into this collection.

We make choices with our eating habits. We don't have to do what we've always done. You can use this cookbook and begin to savor your opportunities to eat. Bon Appetite.

—Edward Espe Brown

Bag Lunch Spread

introduction

The Tassajara Zen Mountain Center, founded in the 1960s, is a year-round Buddhist monastery deep in the Ventana Wilderness near Carmel Valley, California. Tassajara is owned by the San Francisco Zen Center, which also started Green's Restaurant, a very popular vegetarian restaurant (and cookbook) in the San Francisco area. In order to support itself, Tassajara hosts guests and retreats from April to September, offering beautiful and peaceful surroundings complete with hot springs, creek, Japanese bath houses and wonderful food—often the primary reason people visit. And for the Tassajara residents, the guest season abounds with Zen practice opportunities.

In addition to offering three delicious vegetarian meals a day, there is an option to take the Tassajara Bag Lunch. The Bag Lunch allows guests the freedom to hike, go to the swimming pool, creek, or to just relax in the garden. The Bag Lunch offers a gastronomical picnic feast along with a very beautiful visual experience. Each day the Bag Lunch provides as many as twenty different colorful spreads, several roasted vegetables, salads, marinated tofu, cheeses, fresh baked bread, olives, pickles, chutneys and delicious desserts to name just a few.

This book has been created in response to Tassajara guests who have requested the Bag Lunch recipes over the years. These recipes have been adapted from other cookbooks by the Guest Cooks and Bag Lunch Crew at Tassajara. The Guest Cooks and Bag Lunch Crew are Zen residents and students who usually have no formal cooking experience or training, but work in the kitchen as a very important part of their Zen practice. The recipes are quite simple but they have been prepared with great attention and care. This is what makes the food special. The Zen students bring their *zazen* practice (meditation) into their work, taking the leap out of the conditioned small mind, into the freedom and generosity of the mind that is accepting, fresh, and full of possibility. It is the unfettered mind of a beginner, otherwise known as "Beginner's Mind." Cooking as a Zen student is a way to practice generosity, patience, concentration, and thoughtful effort but in Zen, not worrying about the outcome. Here is the paradox—the students have to be concerned with the outcome of the food while not being concerned.

So it being said that if the Zen students cook with a Beginner's Mind, then we all can. And as with any cookbook, the recipes are meant as guidelines. One needs to taste for his or her own and decide as to whether or not a recipe needs more of this or less of that or if it needs an ingredient at all. This is "owning our own reality," as Edward Brown says—cooking for what we want it to be, taking that leap of faith in ourselves.

The Bag Lunch is also a highly creative endeavor, and the Guest Cooks and Bag Lunch Crew are given full creative license to use leftover beans and vegetables—anything left from making the guest meals—to create unique, spur of the moment delicacies, as Edward Brown calls it "The Tassajara Creative Catering Company." This is important given the remoteness of Tassajara, as well as a desire not to waste food. Cooking for the Bag Lunch is also limited, as the ovens and stoves are often in use preparing the guest meals—so little cooking is needed in these recipes.

The food at Tassajara has remained relatively unchanged in many ways since first opening, though it now reflects some of the current eating trends such as more international offerings and exotic food combinations. Since the beginning, Tassajara's cuisine has been built using the same fundamentals

as those at the San Francisco Zen Center's celebrated restaurant, Green's. Tassajara also uses fresh, local organic fruits, vegetables, and herbs whenever possible, high-quality oils and other staples, fresh-ground herbs and spices, and homemade bread.

The ingredients are an important and fundamental part to fine food. Keep this in mind when preparing the recipes in this book. Given the availability of modern conveniences such as canned organic beans, pitted olives, and soup stock pastes, quality doesn't have to be sacrificed to simplify preparation. But more importantly, as Edward Brown says, "the best cooking does not depend on anything more special than the willingness to do the work of putting yourself on the line, on the table. You get to know the ingredients within and without, and how changeable they are, and put them together for everyone to see and, even more revealing, to taste."

This book is a valuable resource for picnics, snacks, appetizers, and "little plates." You'll find an array of finger foods that are easy to put together when there is little time to cook a meal. Many of these recipes can be made in advance as well. It is also a good resource for recipes to use when camping or when traveling. It also provides many ideas for alternatives to those suffering from

allergies, be it dairy, wheat, or soy, and for those desiring to eat fewer carbohydrates or animal products.

As a nutritionist writing this book, there needs to be a word about nutrition. The *Tassajara Cookbook* does include recipes that use high-fat ingredients such as butter and cheeses. And there is always the possibility of substituting some of the lower fat alternatives now available in stores. But keep in mind that variety and moderation are the keys to a healthy diet, a well-known fact when looking at the diets of other cultures such as those in Italy or Asia. Also, the vast majority of the book contains very healthful recipes full of fiber found in the whole grains; essential fatty acids found in the nuts, seeds, and olive oil, and vitamins and minerals found in the fresh organic fruits and vegetables.

I think Julia Child's Diet Plan says it all: "Eat modestly, widely, don't take seconds, and enjoy yourself."

dairy spreads

Orange-Pecan Cream Cheese 19

Olive-Herb Cream Cheese 19

Leek Cream Cheese 20

Feta-Ricotta Herb Spread 20

Trois Fromage (Elanor's Cheese Ball) 23

Artichoke-Walnut Spread 25

Sweet Veggie Tapenade 26

Gorgonzola Spread 28

Fennel Mustard Butter 28

Artichoke Frittata 29

Orange-Pecan Cream Cheese

Orange-Pecan Cream Cheese

Orange zest and orange juice add just a touch of sweetness to this delicious spread. Try it on toasted bagels for breakfast.

½ cup pecans
8 ounces cream cheese, softened
juice of 1 large orange
1½ tablespoons grated orange peel

Toast and chop the pecans. Blend remaining ingredients with a food processor or by hand; stir in pecans. Cover and chill until ready to serve.

MAKES 1½ CUPS

VARIATION: *This recipe can also be whipped until it's light and frothy and served as a dip with fresh fruit.*

Olive-Herb Cream Cheese

Olives and fresh herbs make a wonderful, earthy spread. Use it with roasted vegetables or crisp crackers.

8 ounces cream cheese, softened
2 tablespoons fresh herbs, chopped
¼ teaspoon salt
½ cup olives, niçoise or other black olive, pitted

Blend cream cheese, herbs, salt, and olives with a food processor or by hand; cover and chill until ready to serve.

MAKES 1½ CUPS

Leek Cream Cheese

This makes a very simple, yet elegant spread. Try filling baked mini puff pastry shells for a gourmet treat.

1 bunch leeks, chopped (white parts only)
1 tablespoon butter
1 tablespoon minced garlic
½ cup white wine

½ teaspoon each fresh tarragon, thyme, and oregano
salt and pepper
8 ounces cream cheese, softened

Cut leeks, discarding the tough upper green parts and then wash thoroughly. Saute in butter; when beginning to soften, add garlic, wine, and seasonings. Allow the mixture to cool, and then stir into the cream cheese.

MAKES 2 CUPS

Feta-Ricotta Herb Spread

This makes a fine spread to serve with crackers or bread along with olives, some fresh-grilled vegetables or roasted peppers. Or, serve it along side Sun-Dried Tomato Hummus (see page 59), Baba Ghanoush (see page 33), fresh mint and pita bread to create a Mediterranean feast.

1 cup ricotta cheese
1 cup crumbled feta cheese
2 teaspoons olive oil

¼ cup chopped parsley
2 teaspoons fresh chives or scallions
½ teaspoon dill

Mix all ingredients thoroughly by hand or in a food processor; cover and chill until ready to serve.

MAKES 2 CUPS

VARIATION: *This recipe can also be mixed with any or all of the following ingredients, mixed with a little water, and shaped into a log: sun-dried tomatoes, olives, fresh herbs (great with dill), or fresh mint.*

"When you wash the rice, wash the rice; when you cut the carrots, cut the carrots; when you stir the soup, stir the soup."

—SHUNRYU SUZUKI ROSHI'S ADVICE TO EDWARD BROWN

Trois Fromage
(Elanor's Cheese Ball)

This traditional cheese ball recipe is anything but traditional—serve it as a cheese log covered with toasted nuts or blend it and use it as a spread in a small attractive bowl. Serve with crackers, crudités, or crostini.

6 ounces cream cheese, softened
⅓ cup crumbled blue cheese
1 teaspoon horseradish, or to taste
1 clove garlic, crushed
½ cup grated cheddar cheese
chopped parsley
chopped nuts

Blend one-third of the cream cheese and all of the blue cheese in a food processor. Form this mixture into a log shape on a plate or platter. Next, combine another third of the cream cheese with the horseradish and garlic. Spread this mixture over the first layer. Blend the remaining cream cheese with the grated cheddar cheese. Spread this mixture over the second layer. Garnish or decorate with chopped parsley or nuts. Instead of layering, you can roll the cheese mixture into 2-inch balls and coat with black pepper, minced nuts or fresh herbs. This is best if made a day ahead.

Alternatively, all the ingredients can be combined and blended in a food processor or by hand to make a creamy spread.

MAKES 1 CUP

Artichoke-Walnut Spread

This recipe is one of the most popular spreads offered at the Tassajara Bag Lunch. Its rich, decadent flavor makes an excellent appetizer served with crostini.

½ cup toasted walnuts
½ cup firm silken tofu (or ricotta cheese)
12 artichoke hearts canned in water, drained
¼ cup olive oil
½ cup grated Parmesan, asiago, or a mixture of asiago and provolone cheese
2 tablespoons minced fresh oregano, or other fresh herb
2 cloves garlic, minced
⅓ cup fresh lemon juice, or to taste
salt and pepper

Grind the walnuts in a food processor until fine. If using silken tofu, wrap in a towel and press with a heavy weight for 30 minutes before using. Add the rest of ingredients and blend in the food processor or by hand until chunky but a uniform mixture; cover and chill until ready to serve.

MAKES 2 CUPS

Sweet Veggie Tapenade

This is a wonderful medley of leeks, a colorful trio of bell peppers, and Parmesan cheese. The flavors deepen as it sits.

4 medium leeks, finely chopped (tender white parts only)
1 red bell pepper, finely chopped
1 yellow bell pepper, finely chopped
1 green bell pepper, finely chopped
1 medium yellow onion, finely chopped
1 small red onion, finely chopped
2 tablespoons olive oil
2 tablespoons chopped parsley
¼ cup grated Parmesan or Asiago cheese (optional)
pinch of chili flakes
salt and pepper

Saute leeks, bell peppers, and onions in olive oil until tender. In a medium bowl, combine hot sauteed vegetables with remaining ingredients while stirring to melt the cheese. Add salt and pepper to taste. Serve warm or cold.

MAKES 4 CUPS

Gorgonzola Spread

Blue cheese and juicy red grapes make a stunning combination. Serve this spread with crispy pita triangles, toasted party rye, or crispy garlic-flavored breadsticks for dipping.

½ cup crumbled Gorgonzola, Roquefort, or blue cheese
4 ounces cream cheese, softened
½ cup ricotta cheese
1 teaspoon dry mustard
½ to 1 cup yogurt (depending on desired consistency)

Blend Gorgonzola, cream cheese, ricotta cheese, and dry mustard by hand or in a food processor. Next, add enough yogurt to create a spreadable consistency. Cover and chill until ready to serve.

MAKES 2 CUPS

Fennel Mustard Butter

Serve this delicious, fragrant butter as a spread on sandwiches or roasted fresh vegetables such as asparagus.

1 tablespoon fennel seeds
1 teaspoon chopped fresh rosemary
½ cup butter, at room temperature
1 tablespoon fresh lemon juice
2 teaspoons Dijon mustard
1 clove garlic, minced
salt and pepper

Stir fennel seeds in a small skillet over medium heat until starting to brown, about 1 minute. Place in spice mill and grind to a coarse powder; transfer to a small bowl. Add remaining ingredients to bowl and stir to blend. Season with salt and pepper; cover and chill. This can be made 2 days ahead.

MAKES ½ CUP

Artichoke Frittata

This frittata may be just the recipe for those looking for a high-protein sandwich filling. Just cut into thin slices, top with fresh vegetables, and place on hearty whole-grain bread. This frittata would also be great as a picnic item, with a pile of pickled red onion rings on the side. Using fresh artichokes when in season are delicious but water-packed work just as well.

3 large artichokes
juice of 1 large lemon
3 to 5 tablespoons virgin olive oil, divided
1 large clove garlic, sliced
salt
15 peppercorns, coarsely ground in a mortar
½ cup finely chopped parsley, divided
6 to 8 eggs, lightly beaten
½ cup coarsely grated Romano cheese

Preheat oven to 350 degrees F. If using fresh artichokes, break off the outer leaves and then cut off the top two-thirds of the greens. Trim the outsides, cut the artichokes into quarters, and immediately put them in a bowl with cold water to cover; add the lemon juice. Keep the artichokes in the lemon water until finished slicing to prevent browning. Remove the choke from each piece with a knife. Thinly slice each artichoke quarter into 3 or 4 pieces and return them to the water. Just before cooking, remove the pieces from the water and blot them dry with a towel. If using water-packed artichokes, simply rinse in a colander and slice into quarters.

Heat 2 tablespoons olive oil in an 8-inch frying pan with garlic. When the garlic colors, remove it and then add the artichoke quarters. Give the pan a shake right away to coat the pieces with oil, season with salt and pepper and then add about 2 tablespoons parsley. Saute until the artichokes are browned and thoroughly cooked.

Beat the eggs, season them lightly with salt, and add the remaining parsley, cheese, and cooked artichokes. Oil an 8 x 8-inch baking pan and then pour in the mixture. Bake for about 20 minutes, or until set and slightly browned. Cool thoroughly then slice and serve.

MAKES 1 (8 X 8-INCH) PAN

vegan spreads

Baba Ghanoush 33

Quinoa Caviar 35

Curried Eggplant Spread 36

Roasted Eggplant Compote 38

China Moon Eggplant Spread 39

Roasted Red Bell Pepper Spread 40

Fig and Kalamata Olive Tapenade 43

Black Kalamata Olive Spread 43

Persian Olive, Walnut, and Pomegranate Tapenade 44

Cilantro Pesto 46

Garden of Vegan Tapenade 46

Basil, Lime, and Pumpkin Seed Pesto 48

Basil "Cream" 51

Sun-Dried Tomato Pesto with Walnuts or Almonds 52

Olive, Basil, and Walnut Spread with Madeira 54

Basil, Walnut, and Sun-Dried Tomato Spread 55

Anka's Roasted Red Bell Pepper Spread with Chiles and Lime 56

Nut Butter Spread 56

Tarragon Onion Spread 57

Creamy Tempeh with Garlic and Dill 57

Black Bean Spread 58

Sun-Dried Tomato Hummus 59

Garlic, Cilantro and Chipotle Hummus 61

Sonia's Caper-Garlic Hummus 61

Tempeh Spread with Capers and Onions 62

Rosemary Aioli 63

Vegan Spinach Dip 64

Western-Style Shira-ae 65

Roasted Garlic Dip 66

Creamy Tofu Dip 66

Black Olive Spread with Basil 67

"Zen is not some kind of excitement, but concentration
on our usual everyday routine."

—SHUNRYU SUZUKI ROSHI

Baba Ghanoush

The roasted eggplant gives this spread its sultry and rich flavor. Serve with lavosh or inside fresh pita bread with a bowl of pungent olives.

1 medium eggplant
2 cloves garlic, minced
¼ cup fresh lemon juice
¼ cup sesame tahini
½ teaspoon salt
black pepper
cayenne
pinch of cardamom (optional)
1 tablespoon olive oil
1 tablespoon chopped parsley

Scoop out the eggplant pulp and discard the skin. Place the pulp, garlic, lemon juice, tahini, salt, pepper, cayenne, and cardamom, if using, in a food processor; puree until smooth and then adjust seasonings. To serve, make a trough in the center of the dip and spoon the olive oil into it. Sprinkle with parsley.

MAKES 1½ CUPS

VARIATION:

1 tablespoon olive oil
1 cup minced onion
½ pound mushrooms, minced
½ teaspoon salt
1 teaspoon dill

Heat olive oil and then add remaining ingredients and saute 10 to 15 minutes, or until tender. Stir into pureed eggplant mixture above.

Quinoa Caviar

This caviar is uniquely different and delicious. When cooked, quinoa really does resemble fish eggs, so you may get some puzzled stares or comments from your guests. As a spread, it's an easy way to get some of this super-nutritious quinoa into your diet.

1 eggplant
2 onions, minced
2 cloves garlic, minced
1 tablespoon olive oil
1 cup quinoa
2 cups water
salt and pepper
¼ cup minced cilantro
¼ cup minced parsley
1½ tablespoons soy sauce
2 tablespoons lemon juice

Roast eggplant as described on page 38.

Saute the onions and garlic in olive oil until soft. Stir in the quinoa and lightly toast for 1 minute. Stir in the water and salt to taste; bring to a boil. Reduce heat, cover the pan, and gently simmer the quinoa for 15 minutes. Remove from heat and let stand for 10 minutes. Uncover the pan and fluff the quinoa with a fork; transfer to a bowl and let cool.

Puree the eggplant with the cilantro, parsley, soy sauce, and lemon juice in a food processor. Stir this mixture into the quinoa. Adjust seasoning, adding soy sauce, pepper, or lemon juice to taste. Garnish with sprigs of cilantro and parsley, if desired.

MAKES 4 CUPS

Curried Eggplant Spread

The exotic flavors of curry complement this tasty eggplant salad. Serve it as part of a composed salad plate or with cracker bread or toasted pita. This spread is also good blended with a small amount of yogurt and served as a dip.

1 large eggplant
1 cup diced red bell pepper
1 medium onion, diced
2 tablespoons minced garlic
1 tablespoon olive oil
1 tablespoon minced parsley
1 tablespoon wine vinegar
½ teaspoon salt
¼ teaspoon pepper
1 tablespoon curry powder
juice of 1 lemon

Roast the eggplant and red bell peppers as described on page 38.

Saute onion and garlic in olive oil. Blend in a food processor with eggplant pulp and all other ingredients. Season to taste.

MAKES 4 CUPS

Roasted Eggplant Compote

This is a colorful, light, and easy spread that can be served as part of a composed salad plate, appetizer, or sandwich filling.

1 large eggplant
3 red bell peppers
1 bunch scallions
½ cup balsamic vinegar
½ teaspoon salt
½ teaspoon pepper

Preheat the oven to 400 degrees F. With a sharp knife, make incisions all over the eggplant and place on a lightly oiled baking sheet. Add the peppers to the pan and bake until both are thoroughly soft and wrinkled all over, about 1 hour.

Put the bell peppers in a covered bowl to steam for 10 minutes or so. When peppers and eggplant are cool enough to handle, scrape off the skins and discard.

Puree in a food processor with remaining ingredients until slightly chunky or smooth; adjust seasonings.

MAKES 4 CUPS

Eggplant Spreads

If eggplant is in season, there is no reason to salt before roasting. However, if they're out of season, the eggplants might be bitter. To remove the bitterness, salt them lightly after cutting them open and let stand for about 30 minutes. Rinse and dry thoroughly before proceeding. For roasting eggplant: slice eggplant in half and spread lightly with olive oil. Put on an oiled baking sheet and bake at 450 degrees F for at least 45 minutes, or until tender and the skin is slightly blackened and wrinkled; cool. The large globe eggplant is easier to handle than the narrow Italian or Asian varieties.

China Moon Eggplant Spread

These Asian flavors combined with eggplant make a delicious spread. The sesame oil and brown sugar add depth and sweetness, while freshly grated ginger and dried chili pepper gives the spread a refreshing spiciness. Try rolling in softened rice paper rolls with shredded vegetables. Best if used within a few days. This recipe is from Barbara Tropp, author of the China Moon Cookbook.

  1 large eggplant
  1 tablespoon minced garlic
  ⅓ cup sliced green onions
  1 tablespoon minced ginger
  2 tablespoons minced cilantro
  ½ teaspoon dried chili flakes (or hot chili oil)
  1 tablespoon soy sauce
  1 tablespoon brown sugar
  ½ tablespoon rice vinegar or mirin
  1 tablespoon hot water
  1 tablespoon toasted sesame oil

Roast eggplant as described on page 38.

When the eggplant is cool, scrape pulp off skin and puree in a food processor. Stir together the remaining ingredients except sesame oil. Heat a wok with the sesame oil. When the oil is hot, add the sauce and stir a couple of times. Add pureed eggplant and stir to blend.

MAKES 1 CUP

Roasted Red Bell Pepper Spread

This spread is perfect for garlic lovers. Keep in mind the garlic is raw when adding, so be sure its not too hot. This spread is immensely popular at the Tassajara Bag Lunch.

> 6 red bell peppers, fresh or roasted in jar
> light olive oil, for the peppers
> 4 to 5 cloves garlic
> 1½ tablespoons oil
> 2 teaspoons red wine vinegar
> salt and pepper

Preheat oven to 400 degrees F. Brush the peppers with the light olive oil. Set them on a baking sheet and bake them until the skins are wrinkled and lightly colored, about 40 minutes. Place in a bowl and cover with a plate until cool. When cool, remove the skins and scrape the seeds and ribs from inside.

Mince the peppers and add remaining ingredients. Let sit about 2 hours before serving.

MAKES 3 CUPS

Fig and Kalamata Olive Tapenade

Fig and Kalamata Olive Tapenade

A very simple, yet very exotic tapenade. Serve it with Middle Eastern flat bread, fresh feta cheese, and garlicky olives.

    5 fresh black figs
    1 tablespoon capers, rinsed
    1 tablespoon kalamata olives, pitted
    1 tablespoon olive oil
    2 teaspoons balsamic vinegar

Trim the hard stem end from the figs and then blend everything together in a food processor until smooth; cover and chill. It's best if used that day, but will keep for another day.

MAKES 1 CUP

Black and Kalamata Olive Spread

This is a strong and robust spread and a small amount goes a long way. It's also a good complement to plain hummus—serve them marbled or layered together, or separately with crackers or crostini. Also good in deviled eggs or even on pizza.

    1 cup black olives, pitted
    2 cups kalamata olives, pitted
    ⅓ cup capers, rinsed
    1 tablespoon minced garlic
    1 teaspoon dried basil
    ¼ cup fresh parsley

Blend all ingredients together in a food processor until smooth.

MAKES 2 CUPS

Persian Olive, Walnut, and Pomegranate Tapenade

Middle Eastern dishes often use whole pomegranate seeds in their dishes for wonderful color, flavor, and texture. In this recipe, the seeds burst their sweet-tart flavor into the creamy tapenade. For a real treat, serve it Persian style with a plate of fresh herbs (mint, parsley, dill, and scallions), a chunk of feta cheese, cucumber slices, and pita or traditional Middle Eastern flat bread.

1 cup unseasoned green olives, such as Picholines, pitted
⅔ cup toasted walnuts, finely chopped
½ cup whole pomegranate seeds
¼ cup chopped cilantro
1 clove minced garlic
2 tablespoons extra virgin olive oil
lemon juice
salt
2 pita rounds, cut into triangles

Finely mince the olives. In a bowl, combine the olives, walnuts, pomegranate seeds, cilantro, garlic, and olive oil; stir to mix. Add a few drops of lemon juice and salt if necessary. The mixture may not need salt if the olives are salty.

Preheat the oven to 375 degrees F. Toast the pita triangles on a baking sheet until lightly colored and crisp, about 8 to 10 minutes; let cool. Serve tapenade with the pita toasts.

MAKES 1½ CUPS

Cilantro Pesto

This is creamy, rich pesto for cilantro lovers. Its bright green color and fresh flavor will enhance any sandwich. Try making a Mexican pizza or burrito with queso fresco, black beans, fresh chiles, and tomatoes. Or use it with other pestos with pasta or vegetable toppings.

> 2 cloves garlic
> ½ cup raw almonds
> 1 bunch cilantro
> 3 tablespoons lemon juice
> ¾ cup olive oil
> ½ teaspoon salt

Place all ingredients in a food processor in the order listed above and blend until smooth. If you want it more or less chunky, decrease or increase the proportions of lemon juice and oil, but always kept the ratio of 3 parts oil to 1 part lemon juice.

MAKES 1 CUP

Garden of Vegan Tapenade

This very rich tapenade can be topped on slices of crispy potatoes, cucumber slices, or even hard-boiled eggs for a wonderful appetizer. For lunch, try it on rye crisp crackers or whole-grain bread.

> 1 cup kalamata olives, pitted
> 2 cloves garlic, minced
> 10 to 12 sun-dried tomatoes, rehydrated
> ¼ cup capers, rinsed
> 1 cup olive oil
> 2 tablespoons Bragg's Liquid Aminos or tamari

Blend all ingredients together until coarse in a food processor.

MAKES 1 CUP

Cilantro Pesto

Basil, Lime, and Pumpkin Seed Pesto

This is an excellent pesto packed with nutrition and fiber. The freshness of the lime and basil are a great complement to the rich, nutty flavor of pumpkin seeds.

  1 cup raw pumpkin seeds
  1 cup basil, packed
  4 tablespoons lime juice
  3 cloves garlic
  2 tablespoons olive oil
  salt and pepper

Lightly toast pumpkin seeds and grind until they stick to the walls of the food processor. Add the remaining ingredients. Add more olive oil or lime juice to thin if necessary.

MAKES 1 CUP

Basil "Cream"

Basil "Cream"

Basil and cashews make a wonderful combination to create a rich, creamy spread. Make this spread at the height of summer when fresh basil is available. Serve in place of mayonnaise or mustard on sandwiches, with grilled vegetables and tofu, or even on pasta!

1 cup cashews
9 to 10 cups fresh basil
¼ cup lemon juice
1 tablespoon miso
olive oil
pepper
4 to 5 fresh spinach leaves

Grind cashews in a food processor. Add basil, lemon juice, and miso and then blend until smooth. Add olive oil and pepper as needed to make a creamy consistency, and add the fresh spinach leaves to help keep the color vibrant and bright.

MAKES 1 CUP

Sun-Dried Tomato Pesto with Walnuts or Almonds

The intense flavor of sun-dried tomatoes and the tartness of lemon juice create a striking balance. Try spreading it over cream cheese or goat cheese on crackers, crostini, or breads. As with other pestos, it can also be served on pasta, grilled vegetables, baked potatoes, or even pizza.

    1 cup sun-dried tomatoes
    1 clove garlic
    ½ cup walnuts or almonds
    2 tablespoons fresh lemon juice
    ½ cup extra virgin olive oil
    2 tablespoons each fresh basil, oregano, and dill (or 1 teaspoon each dried)

Steam or simmer the sun-dried tomatoes until soft. In a food processor, add the garlic, sun-dried tomatoes, and nuts. Add remaining ingredients and process until smooth.

MAKES 1 CUP

Olive, Basil, and Walnut Spread with Madeira

The sharp flavor of pimiento-stuffed olives is mellowed here by the other ingredients, creating a tantalizing pesto-like spread. It can launch any Greek or Italian menu with real gusto. If you want to serve it with crackers, choose some that are plain and simple so they don't compete with the flavor of the spread.

1 cup pimiento-stuffed olives, drained
⅔ cup chopped basil leaves
½ cup raw walnuts
¼ cup Madeira or dry sherry
1 tablespoon fresh lemon juice
2 cloves garlic, minced
several grinds of pepper

Puree all the ingredients together in a food processor until thick and fairly homogenous. Prepare the spread well ahead of time, if possible, so the flavors have time to blend. Cover and chill; can be stored in the refrigerator for up to a week, but return to room temperature before serving.

MAKES 1½ CUPS

Basil, Walnut, and Sun-Dried Tomato Spread

This is a rich, flavorful spread and a little goes a long way. It's a great complement to grilled vegetables and baked potatoes. Or, simply combine it with yogurt to serve as a dip.

1 cup sun-dried tomatoes
3 cloves garlic
3 tablespoons lemon juice
1 cup raw walnuts
1 cup fresh basil
1 teaspoon dried oregano
1 teaspoon dried dill
1 cup olive oil

Steam or simmer the sun-dried tomatoes until soft. Place all the ingredients in a food processor and blend until smooth.

MAKES 2½ CUPS

Anka's Roasted Red Bell Pepper Spread with Chiles and Lime

This southwest-inspired recipe was created by Anka, the head of the Bag Lunch Crew one summer at Tassajara. It's a delicious low-fat and colorful spread.

5 red bell peppers, roasted
2 tablespoons lime juice
1½ tablespoons olive oil
1 serrano chile, seeded and minced
½ cup chopped cilantro
salt and pepper

Roast bell peppers as described on page 38 and then dice. Combine the peppers with the remaining ingredients and mix by hand.

MAKES 2 CUPS

VARIATION: *Instead of serrano chiles, use 2 tablespoons rinsed capers and a pinch of cayenne.*

Nut Butter Spread

This Bag Lunch favorite has lots of protein, essential fats and minerals—sort of a super nutritious peanut butter! It is hand mixed to keep its chunky texture. Try it spread on celery for "ants on a log" with raisins.

⅓ cup sunflower seeds, lightly toasted
⅓ cup sesame seeds, lightly toasted
⅓ cup cashews, toasted and chopped
2 cups peanut butter
1 cup tahini
1 teaspoon honey

Mix thoroughly until well combined. Use in place of peanut or other butters on bread and crackers.

MAKES 2 CUPS

Tarragon Onion Spread

This mixture of onion, lemon, and fresh tarragon creates a delicious, vibrant spread. It can be used as a dip or spread, especially with marinated tofu and roasted vegetables. To use as a dip, thin with water or lemon juice.

1 tablespoon olive oil

1 onion, minced

5 cloves garlic, minced

2 tablespoons fresh tarragon

2 bay leaves

¼ cup lemon juice

½ teaspoon salt

black pepper

1 cup water

Heat the olive oil in a saute pan and then add onion and garlic; cook until soft, about 5 minutes. Add tarragon and bay leaves and cook 5 minutes more. Add remaining ingredients and cook about 15 minutes, stirring occasionally, until mixture is very thick. Remove bay leaves and blend mixture in a food processor to create a creamy texture.

MAKES ABOUT 1 CUP

Creamy Tempeh with Garlic and Dill

Lemon, garlic, and herbs are the perfect complement to tempeh in this delicious spread.

6 ounces tempeh

¼ cup oil

2 tablespoons lemon juice or apple cider vinegar

½ teaspoon salt

½ cup water

1 clove garlic, minced

¼ teaspoon dill

2 tablespoons parsley

Cut the tempeh into 1 x 1-inch pieces and steam for 20 minutes. Combine all the ingredients except the parsley in a food processor and blend until smooth. Garnish with the parsley and serve chilled.

MAKES 1½ CUPS

Black Bean Spread

This spread/dip is very easy to prepare. Try using it on crispy corn tortillas or chips, or serve with Monterey Jack or cheddar cheese, a little sour cream and roasted red bell pepper.

    2 cups cooked black beans
    1 small red onion, minced
    3 tablespoons minced cilantro
    1 clove garlic, minced
    1 teaspoon herb mixture*
    1 teaspoon cumin
    2 teaspoons lime juice
    ¼ teaspoon salt

Place all ingredients together in a food processor and blend until smooth.

MAKES 2 CUPS

Herb mixture: Equal amounts of oregano, paprika, and cayenne ground in a spice mill.

Sun-Dried Tomato Hummus

Toasted sesame tahini and sun-dried tomatoes give this traditional Middle Eastern spread an especially rich flavor and bright color. Try it on celery, cucumber slices, or zucchini instead of bread.

2 cups chickpeas (garbanzo beans), soaked overnight
¼ teaspoon salt
6 to 8 sun-dried tomatoes, rehydrated
¾ cup tahini
3 cloves garlic, minced
2 tablespoons lemon juice or apple cider vinegar
¼ cup olive oil
1 tablespoon Bragg's Liquid Aminos or tamari
1 teaspoon cumin
½ teaspoon salt
¼ teaspoon cayenne pepper

Drain the chickpeas and then cover them generously with fresh water; bring to a boil. Lower the heat to a slow boil, add ¼ teaspoon salt, and cook until the beans are completely soft, about 1½ hours, or more. Other alternatives are to cook the chickpeas in a pressure cooker or to use 1 (12-ounce) can. If using canned, be sure to rinse well before using.

Drain the chickpeas and put in a food processor with the sun-dried tomatoes, tahini, garlic, lemon juice, olive oil, Bragg's, cumin, ½ teaspoon salt, and cayenne pepper; process until smooth. Extra liquid may be necessary to thin; use the cooking liquid from the beans, water, or additional olive oil. Taste and adjust the salt, lemon, and oil to your liking.

MAKES 3 CUPS

"There is nothing more zen than careful observation of the
obvious. If you keep practicing that, you'll figure it out."

—EDWARD ESPE BROWN

Garlic, Cilantro and Chipotle Hummus

This is a delicious, spicy hummus. Serve on Middle Eastern flatbread or try with tortilla chips along with guacamole.

1½ cups cooked chickpeas
3 tablespoons tahini
½ cup fresh-squeezed lemon juice
½ to 1 teaspoon canned chipotle, or to taste
½ cup chopped cilantro
3 cloves garlic, minced
½ teaspoon salt

Combine chickpeas and tahini in a small bowl and cream together or put in a food processor and puree. Add the remaining ingredients and blend until smooth and creamy. Add water to thin if necessary and add salt to taste. Garnish with fresh cilantro and minced chipotle.

MAKES 2 CUPS

Sonia's Caper-Garlic Hummus

This hummus shows how versatile hummus can be. It is delicious and attractive given the addition of whole capers. Keep in mind it will be salty with the capers, so be careful when adding more salt.

1½ cups cooked chickpeas
3 tablespoons tahini
½ cup fresh-squeezed lemon juice
2 tablespoons capers, rinsed
3 cloves garlic, minced
salt

Combine chickpeas, tahini, and lemon juice in a small bowl and cream together or put in a food processor and puree. Add the remaining ingredients by hand and mix well.

MAKES 2 CUPS

Tempeh Spread
with Capers and Onions

The pungent lemon and caper flavors add vibrancy to this creamy spread. Try this spread rolled up in lavosh or on crispy crackers.

6 ounces tempeh
½ cup water
1 bay leaf
1 tablespoon tamari
2 tablespoons capers, drained
2 green onions, minced
¼ cup chopped celery
¼ cup mayonnaise (regular or vegan)
1 tablespoon fresh lemon juice

In a saute pan, combine tempeh, water, bay leaf, and tamari and simmer for 20 minutes. Cool and drain the tempeh and then grate. Mix tempeh with remaining ingredients. The mixture should be a spreading consistency; cover and chill until ready to serve.

MAKES 2 CUPS

Rosemary Aioli

The rich and creamy flavor of this non-dairy spread comes from the rosemary-infused oil. Use it in place of butter on grilled vegetables or bread.

3 sprigs fresh rosemary
¼ cup olive oil
3 teaspoons fresh rosemary, or more to taste
3 cloves garlic
2 tablespoons fresh lemon juice, or more to taste
2 (12-ounce) blocks soft tofu
salt

To make the rosemary-infused oil, place washed sprigs of fresh rosemary in a clean jar and pour in the olive oil. Let sit for a few days in the refrigerator until the flavor is strong enough. Remove and discard the herbs. Keep oil covered in the refrigerator. This will keep for up to several months if not used right away.

To finish the spread, blend the rosemary-infused oil with all the remaining ingredients in a food processor until smooth. Taste and adjust seasonings. The rosemary flavor should be very strong.

MAKES 2 CUPS

Vegan Spinach Dip

Try serving this dip with pita bread or sliced raw vegetables, or use as a sandwich filling.

1 pound fresh spinach
8 ounces water chestnuts
1 cup Tofu Mayonnaise (see page 92)
10 ounces silken tofu
2 tablespoons grated onion
2 cloves garlic, minced
1 teaspoon basil
2 teaspoons tarragon
2 teaspoons dill weed
1 tablespoon minced parsley
1 ¼ teaspoons salt, or to taste
½ teaspoon black pepper

Wash and cook spinach until wilted; drain and squeeze dry. Dice water chestnuts and set aside. Combine remaining ingredients in a food processor and process until well combined.

Stir together the spinach, water chestnuts, and tofu mixture. Refrigerate for several hours or overnight.

MAKES 4 CUPS

Western-Style Shira-ae

This salad makes an unusual, yet delicious high-protein spread or sandwich filling.

6 ounces soft tofu, mashed
1 tablespoon tahini
1 tablespoon lemon juice
1½ tablespoons rice vinegar
½ teaspoon salt or 1 tablespoon red miso
1 teaspoon sake or white wine
1 cucumber or small carrot, cut into thin rounds
2 hard-boiled eggs, chopped
¼ cup chopped walnuts
¼ cup raisins
2 tablespoons cucumber pickles, minced (optional)

Combine first six ingredients in a food processor and blend until smooth. Gently stir in the remaining ingredients and serve immediately.

MAKES 2 CUPS

Roasted Garlic Dip

Roasting garlic gives it a rich and buttery consistency. And using this roasted garlic dip is delicious and rich in protein.

¾ cup soft or silken tofu, drained
2 tablespoons apple cider vinegar
1 tablespoon maple syrup
½ teaspoon salt
pinch black pepper
6 cloves roasted garlic
½ onion, diced
1 to 2 teaspoons olive oil

Combine all ingredients in a food processor and blend until smooth and creamy.

MAKES 1 CUP

Creamy Tofu Dip

Serve this dip with a platter of celery and carrot sticks, sliced jicama, whole green beans, cucumbers, cherry tomatoes, and Jerusalem artichokes.

10 ounces soft tofu
½ cup oil
2 tablespoons lemon juice
1½ tablespoons honey
¼ cup chopped parsley
2 tablespoons minced dill pickles
1 tablespoon minced onion
½ teaspoon mustard
½ teaspoon salt

Combine all ingredients together in a food processor and blend until smooth.

MAKES ABOUT 2 CUPS

Black Olive Spread with Basil

Delicious olives combined with fresh basil—what could be better?

1 cup black olives, pitted
1½ tablespoons capers
1 clove garlic
Juice of 1 lemon
4 tablespoons olive oil
Fresh ground pepper, to taste
2 tablespoons minced fresh basil
½ teaspoon sugar (optional)

Combine all ingredients in a food processor and blend until smooth. If too salty, add optional sugar. Taste and adjust seasonings.

MAKES ABOUT 1 CUP

pâtés & loaves

Almond Pâté

This recipe is from The Tassajara Recipe Book *by Edward Brown. This savory, flavorful nut pâté claims the distinction of being possibly the most requested recipe during the guest season. Tassajara uses it as a sandwich spread and as an ingredient in the Nut Loaf (see page 81). Try this pâté as a filling for mushrooms, or as a "nut chutney" for grains or vegetables.*

    1 cup minced onion
    1 tablespoon butter
    ½ teaspoon freshly ground cumin
    ½ teaspoon savory
    ½ teaspoon fine herbs
    1 cup raw almonds, ground fairly fine
    ½ cup plus 2 tablespoons toasted breadcrumbs
    2 tablespoons minced parsley
    1 teaspoon tamari
    1 small clove garlic, minced
    salt and fresh-ground pepper
    2 to 4 tablespoons mayonnaise or sour cream
    lemon slices

Cook the onion in the butter over low heat with the cumin, savory, and fine herbs until they are soft.

Scrape the onion mixture into a bowl. Using your fingers, work in the almonds, breadcrumbs, parsley, tamari, and garlic. Taste and season with salt and pepper.

Gradually mix in the mayonnaise or sour cream until the mixture holds together. Shape it into a log or press into a serving bowl and garnish with overlapping slices of lemon.

MAKES 2 CUPS

Mushroom Pâté

This is a rich, full-flavored pâté that can be served as a snack, appetizer, or for picnics.

1 red onion, finely chopped
2 cloves garlic, minced
2 cups finely chopped mushrooms
1 cup red wine
1 tablespoon nutritional yeast

1 teaspoon dried herbs (for example, sage, thyme, rosemary, nutmeg)
salt and pepper
1 cup toasted walnuts

Saute the onion, garlic, and mushrooms in red wine until all the moisture has evaporated.

Remove from heat and add nutritional yeast, herbs, and salt and pepper to taste. In a food processor, grind the walnuts, then add the cooked mixture and blend until smooth. Cool and spoon into a bowl to serve; garnish with a few toasted walnuts.

MAKES 3 CUPS

Mushroom-Almond Pâté

This pâté was a very popular recipe that guests often asked for and, in fact, was given to Tassajara by a guest. It was originally made with breadcrumbs but guest cooks replaced them with almond meal to increase the nutritional value. For a high-fiber pâté, one can substitute oat bran for the almond meal.

1 to 2 cloves garlic, minced
1 small yellow onion, finely chopped
4 to 5 tablespoons butter
¾ pound mushrooms, finely chopped
¼ cup cooking sherry or Marsala

¾ teaspoon salt
½ teaspoon ground thyme
⅛ teaspoon white pepper
1 cup finely ground almonds

Saute garlic and onion in 4 tablespoons butter until translucent. Add mushrooms and cook until soft. Add more butter if needed (the butter gives the pâté-like texture) and cook off any remaining liquid. Add sherry and cook off the alcohol. Taste and adjust seasoning with salt, thyme, and white pepper; add the almond meal. Cool and then put into bowls, mounding attractively.

MAKES 2 CUPS

Mushroom Pâté

Asian Walnut Pâté

A great sandwich spread served with alfalfa sprouts, or use as a dip for vegetables or crispy pita wedges.

1 cup ground walnuts
1 pound firm tofu, drained and crumbled
2 cloves garlic, minced
2 tablespoons toasted sesame oil
2 tablespoons tahini
3 tablespoons yellow white miso
2 teaspoons umeboshi plum paste
3 tablespoons Tofu Mayonnaise (see page 88)
3 tablespoons maple syrup
juice of 2 lemons
⅛ teaspoon cayenne, or to taste
¼ cup minced parsley
¼ cup chopped pimientos

Combine all ingredients together, except parsley and pimientos, in a food processor and process until very smooth. Transfer to a large bowl and then stir in parsley and pimientos.

MAKES 4 CUPS

Savory Sunflower Pâté

This earthy pâté is rich in flavor and nutrition.

1 medium onion, coarsely chopped
½ cup virgin olive oil, divided
½ cup warm water
¼ cup tamari
1 to 2 large potatoes, peeled and diced
1 cup raw, shelled sunflower seeds
½ cup whole wheat flour
½ cup nutritional yeast
1 to 2 cloves garlic
1½ teaspoons dried herbs (for example, sage, basil, oregano, marjoram, thyme)

Preheat oven to 350 degrees F. Saute onion in 1 tablespoon olive oil until soft. Add onion and all other ingredients to a food processor and blend until very smooth. The mixture needs to be very thick to hold its shape.

Pour mixture into two greased loaf pans and bake until set, about 1 hour; cool thoroughly. Once cooled, loosen the loaves from the pan with a table knife and then remove carefully. Wrap in plastic wrap and store in the refrigerator for up to 2 weeks, or freeze up to 3 months.

MAKES 2 LOAVES

VARIATION: *Add ½ to 1 cup chopped cilantro or parsley with 1 cup dried breadcrumbs or rolled oats to mixture.*

Pâté Tempeh

Serve this hearty spread with seed crackers, crostini, or toasted pita triangles.

1 cup slivered almonds
1 small onion, minced
1 clove garlic, minced
½ pound mushrooms, sliced
2 tablespoons olive oil
8 ounces tempeh
1 teaspoon tamari
½ teaspoon each thyme and sage
salt

Preheat oven to 350 degrees F. Spread almonds on a baking sheet in one layer and bake until golden, about 10 minutes. Saute the onion, garlic, and mushrooms in oil until soft. Cut the tempeh into ½-inch cubes and add to the mushroom mixture.

Add tamari, thyme, sage, and salt to taste. Cook mixture about 15 minutes, or until most of the liquid has evaporated.

In a food processor or blender, grind the almonds. Add the remaining ingredients and process until the pâté is thick and smooth. Cover and chill; will keep about 1 week.

MAKES 2 CUPS

Parisienne Pâté

An Asian-inspired French pâté—a delectable dish for guests. Serve with crackers or thin slices of toast.

8 ounces tempeh, cut in half
1 cup vegetable stock
1 bay leaf
2 cups cubed sourdough bread (½-inch cubes)
2 tablespoons olive oil
1 medium onion, chopped
2 tablespoons tamari
1 tablespoon mirin
½ teaspoon marjoram
½ teaspoon thyme
½ teaspoon nutmeg

Heat oven to 350 degrees F. In a medium saucepan, simmer the tempeh halves in vegetable stock with bay leaf for 10 minutes. Remove bay leaf and tempeh.

Add more stock to the saucepan, enough to make ¾ cup, and bread cubes and let soak. Heat olive oil and saute onion until soft. After the tempeh has cooled, grate.

In a food processor (or you can mash by hand), combine the grated tempeh, soaked bread, onion, and remaining ingredients; blend until smooth. Pack mixture into a lightly oiled 1-quart ovenproof bowl. Cover bowl with foil and place in a pan of hot water. Bake for 30 minutes, remove cover, and bake another 20 to 30 minutes. Cool, unmold onto a plate, and garnish with fresh herbs.

MAKES 3 CUPS

"When you are practicing, you realize that your mind is like a screen. If the screen is colorful, colorful enough to attract people, then it will not serve its purpose. So to have a screen which is not colorful—to have a pure, plain white screen—is the most important point."

—SHUNRYU SUZUKI ROSHI

Three Nut Pâté

This is another favorite of the Tassajara guests. Fresh basil makes a wonderful addition to this pâté. This recipe is best if made ahead and allowed to sit a few hours before serving for the flavor to develop.

½ cup each almonds, cashews, and walnuts
1 onion, coarsely chopped
½ cup sliced scallions
1 tablespoon minced garlic
¼ teaspoon allspice
½ teaspoon dried thyme
1 bay leaf
2 tablespoons olive oil
¼ cup red wine
2 tablespoons soy sauce
½ cup chopped fresh basil
¼ cup dried breadcrumbs
¾ cup firm tofu, crumbled (optional)*
salt and pepper

Preheat the oven to 350 degrees F. Spread the nuts in one layer on a baking sheet and toast for 10 to 15 minutes until golden brown. Then grind the nuts to a fine powder; set aside.

Saute the onion, scallions, garlic, allspice, thyme, and bay leaf in olive oil until soft. Add red wine and soy sauce and cook until almost dry. Add basil to onion mixture and continue cooking until well combined. Add breadcrumbs, tofu, if desired, and salt and pepper to taste. Blend mixture together in a food processor. Spoon into a serving dish and garnish with fresh basil leaves.

MAKES 2 CUPS

If using tofu, increase breadcrumbs to 1 cup.

The Nut Loaf

This very popular nut loaf requested by guests at Tassajara for the last 25 years was originally published in The Tassajara Recipe Book *by Edward Brown. It's a good way to use any leftover cheese you may have accumulated. The type of cheese you can use is flexible, but try to include some strongly-flavored cheese such as Brie, Gorgonzola, Gruyère, or Smoked Gouda. When making the Almond Pâté, double the recipe so there is some for this nut loaf. It took some tinkering to produce a loaf that did not crumble to pieces upon removal from the pan, or later upon slicing.*

1½ cups sliced mushrooms

2 cloves garlic, minced

1 green bell pepper, diced

½ teaspoon each thyme, oregano, marjoram, tarragon, and basil

½ teaspoon salt

¼ teaspoon pepper

2 tablespoons olive oil or butter

2 cups cooked brown rice or 2 cups dried breadcrumbs

4 eggs

1 cup Almond Pâté (see page 71)

½ cup toasted cashews

1 cup ricotta cheese (or cottage cheese or yogurt)

1 cup grated mixed cheese (see recipe introduction)

2 tablespoons minced parsley

Preheat oven to 350 degrees F. Saute mushrooms, garlic, bell pepper, and seasonings in olive oil or butter until tender. If using breadcrumbs instead of rice, toast 4 slices bread until brown, cool slightly, and then grind in a food processor until fine.

Beat eggs in a large bowl, then stir in all remaining ingredients. Add enough ricotta or cottage cheese so that the mixture binds together firmly. Add more grated cheese and herbs to taste—the mixture should taste strong and savory.

Thoroughly grease two loaf pans. Put nut loaf into pans, smoothing the top with a spatula. Bake for approximately 1 hour. Loaves should be golden brown and firm to the touch. Be sure to not overcook or they will tend to be dry. Let sit for 5 to 10 minutes; then turn out on a wire rack to cool. The loaves freeze well for up to 1 month.

MAKES 2 LOAVES

Jesse's "Lighter-Less Dairy" Loaf

This recipe is similar to The Nut Loaf on page 77, but a lighter version adapted by a student.

2 tablespoons olive oil
1½ cups chopped onions
1 teaspoon dried sage
½ teaspoon dried thyme
2 cups sliced mushrooms
1 cup roasted cashews, chopped
1 cup roasted walnuts, chopped
1 teaspoon tamari
salt and pepper
1 cup cooked brown rice
1 cup grated carrots
½ cup grated cheddar cheese
2 eggs, beaten
1 cup dried breadcrumbs
dried chili pepper flakes (optional)

Heat oven to 350 degrees F. Heat olive oil over medium heat. Saute the onions with herbs until translucent; add the mushrooms, cashews, and walnuts and saute until they start to stick to the bottom of the pan and are nicely browned. Add the tamari and salt and pepper to taste.

In a large bowl, combine the rice, carrots, and onion mixture and combine until well mixed. Add the cheese, eggs, breadcrumbs, and chili flakes, if desired, to taste.

Generously grease two loaf pans and fill with loaf mixture. Bake for 1 hour, or until the tops are slightly golden. Serve with mushroom gravy if desired.

MAKES 2 LOAVES

Vegetable-Walnut Pâté

Guests love this pâté and seem to think it tastes like real chopped liver . . .

1 tablespoon olive oil
½ cup minced onion
½ teaspoon salt
1½ cups chopped green beans
2 hard-boiled eggs (optional)
¼ cup chopped walnuts
1 to 2 tablespoons white wine or 2 teaspoons lemon juice
1 to 2 tablespoons mayonnaise
½ cup chopped parsley
pepper

Heat oil in a small skillet. Add onion and salt and saute over medium heat until onion begins to brown, about 10 minutes. Add the green beans and saute until tender.

Combine all ingredients together in a food processor and blend until a smooth paste forms. Spoon into a serving dish.

MAKES 3 CUPS

tofu, tempeh & egg salad sandwich fillings

Herb-Crusted Tofu

This recipe is from Vegetarian Cooking for Everyone *by Deborah Madison.*

16 ounces firm tofu
1 cup dried breadcrumbs
½ cup grated Parmesan or asiago cheese
1 tablespoon chopped parsley
1 teaspoon dried basil or marjoram
½ teaspoon dried thyme
½ teaspoon dried savory
1 egg, beaten with 2 tablespoons milk or soy milk
olive oil for frying

Slice the tofu into about ⅓-inch-thick pieces, then across to form triangles. Set the triangles on paper towels to drain. Meanwhile, combine the breadcrumbs, cheese, and herbs in a shallow dish. Dip each tofu triangle into the egg mixture and then the breadcrumb mixture, coating both sides.

Film a skillet with olive oil. When hot, add the tofu and fry on both sides over medium heat until golden and crisp, about 10 to 12 minutes.

MAKES ABOUT 18 TRIANGLES

Happy Tuna Salad

This is a very simple and delicious salad spread. Kids will love it. Serve it on bread, lettuce, or use it to stuff vegetables such as celery.

8 ounces tempeh
1 cup diced celery
¼ cup sliced scallions
¼ cup sweet pickle relish
2 tablespoons minced parsley
½ cup mayonnaise

Steam tempeh for 20 minutes; cool and grate. Put the grated tempeh and remaining ingredients together in a bowl and mix well. Chill several hours before serving.

MAKES 1½ CUPS

Egg Salad

This recipe makes great egg salad and was found in Secrets to Making Egg Salad *by "The Egg Maker" at Tassajara one season.*

To cook eggs, put a few inches of cold water in a saucepan, add a few pinches of salt and bring to a boil. Reduce heat to a simmer, then carefully add eggs making one layer. Cover and cook 20 minutes; cool with cold water. If the water warms up from the eggs, drain and replace with more cold water—this is essential for helping the eggs to peel easier later.

Use an egg slicer to chop the eggs once peeled. Constants in egg salad are chopped celery and a smaller amount of some kind of onion—green, red, or white will work. Shallots are also nice. Other constants are mayonnaise (or nayonnaise), salt, pepper, and Dijon or stone-ground mustard. Tassajara's most common recipe was simply to add sweet pickle relish to the above. Adding yogurt and curry powder is also tasty. Other popular additions are fresh or dried dill, other fresh minced herbs, cumin, chopped olives, sun-dried tomatoes, or chopped almonds.

Eggless Egg Salad

This unique salad has lots of texture, nutrition, and rich flavor from the sesame and peanut oils. It can be used the same as any egg salad—in pita, on bread, crackers, or greens.

12 ounces firm tofu
3 scallions, minced
1 medium carrot, coarsely grated
1 stalk celery, finely minced
⅓ cup toasted sunflower seeds

1 teaspoon grated ginger
Tofu Mayonnaise (see page 92)
salt and fresh-ground pepper
tamari sauce

Cut the tofu into a bowl in ½-inch cubes. Add the scallions, carrot, celery, sunflower seeds, and ginger and then mix gently. Add the Tofu Mayonnaise, season to taste with the salt, pepper, and tamari sauce, and mix once again. Chill until ready to serve.

MAKES 2½ CUPS

No Egg Salad

This eggless salad spread is more traditional and has less fat than the Eggless Egg Salad. Try this mixture on pumpernickel bread topped with alfalfa sprouts.

12 ounces firm tofu, mashed
¼ teaspoon tumeric
1 stalk celery, chopped
¼ cup minced onion
1½ tablespoons mayonnaise

1 tablespoon minced parsley
½ teaspoon dried dill
½ teaspoon salt
¼ teaspoon dry mustard
¼ teaspoon celery seed

Combine all ingredients in a bowl and mix well. Chill for about 1 hour before serving.

MAKES 2 CUPS

Tofu Salad Sandwich Spread

From the Green's Cookbook: *"This salad has been on the Green's Restaurant menu since it opened. The tofu is seasoned with fresh herbs, mustard, capers, scallions, and finely diced vegetables, which also give it texture. This is a light, moist, satisfying sandwich filling, especially good on whole wheat bread." The version below has had some creative input from Tassajara's guest cooks. I've also made this using wasabi mayonnaises and received rave reviews.*

18 ounces firm tofu
5 tablespoons finely diced red bell pepper
5 tablespoons finely diced celery
4 tablespoons finely diced carrot
2 tablespoons minced red onions
2 tablespoons finely chopped fresh herbs: parsley, thyme, marjoram, and savory
½ cup mayonnaise or 5 tablespoons sesame oil
1½ tablespoons Dijon mustard
1 teaspoon red wine vinegar or sherry vinegar
tamari
salt and pepper

Rinse the tofu in cool water. To dry and crumble the tofu, place it in a clean towel, gather the corners together, and twist the towel around it until all the water has been squeezed out. Put the tofu in a bowl with the vegetables, herbs, mayonnaise or sesame oil, Dijon mustard and vinegar. Lightly mix everything together with a fork and then season with tamari, salt, and pepper. Although the taste may be bland at first, the flavors of the vegetables and herbs will strengthen and gradually permeate the salad as it sits. If possible, let it sit at least 30 minutes before using.

MAKES 3 CUPS

Mexican Tempeh Salad

This is a delicious variation to other tempeh, or tofu salads and children love it! Try adding some chipotle chiles for extra heat.

1 cup vegetable stock	2 tablespoons minced cilantro
½ cup tamari	½ cup salsa
8 ounces tempeh	⅓ cup mayonnaise
½ cup minced yellow onion	1 tablespoon fresh lemon juice
2 medium tomatoes, diced and drained well	salt and pepper

Combine the vegetable stock and tamari in a saucepan. Add the tempeh and simmer for 20 minutes; drain. After the tempeh has cooled, grate, and then combine with remaining ingredients; mix well. Chill 1 hour before serving.

MAKES 2½ CUPS

VARIATION: *Try adding chipotle chiles. They are available canned for easy use. But remember, a little goes a long way.*

Tofu Mayonnaise

This is a homemade, non-dairy alternative to mayonnaise, otherwise known as Nayonniase.

6 ounces soft tofu
1½ to 2 tablespoons fresh lemon juice
2 tablespoons oil
½ teaspoon salt or 1 tablespoon red miso
black pepper, to taste

Combine all ingredients in a food processor and blend until smooth.

MAKES ABOUT 1 CUP

For a variety of mayonnaise flavors try adding some of these variations to the recipe above: Add ¼ cup diced onion; curry powder; 1 teaspoon chipotle chiles; fresh grated gingerroot; dill and garlic; diced celery and onion; 2 tablespoons tahini; miso; ¼ cup chopped leeks; dried herbs, such as oregano, marjoram, sorrel, and caraway.

Mexican Tempeh Salad

Tempeh Salad

This is a tempeh version of tuna salad. For a variation, use tempeh made with hijiki and add fresh dill.

1 cup vegetable stock
½ cup tamari
8 ounces tempeh
¾ cup chopped celery
¼ cup chopped dill pickles
½ cup minced red, yellow, or green onions
⅓ cup mayonnaise
1 tablespoon fresh lemon juice
¼ teaspoon pepper
paprika

Combine the vegetable stock and tamari in a saucepan. Add tempeh and simmer for 20 minutes; drain. After the tempeh has cooled, grate and then combine with remaining ingredients; mix well. Sprinkle with paprika and chill 1 hour before serving.

MAKES 2½ CUPS

Tofu "Bits"
in Kosho's Secret Tenzo Sauce

Tofu Bacon Bits? Looks like this sauce isn't a "secret" anymore! Great with split pea soup or as a salad topping.

SECRET TENZO SAUCE
- ½ cup tamari
- ⅓ cup mirin
- ¼ cup honey
- 2 tablespoons sesame oil
- ½ teaspoon dry mustard

32 ounces firm tofu

Preheat oven to 300 degrees F.

Combine all the ingredients for the Secret Tenzo Sauce. Crumble the tofu and toss with the sauce. Bake for 2 to 3 hours, stirring now and then. The "bits" are done when they are crunchy and granular.

MAKES 3 CUPS

chutneys, sauces & salsas

Pineapple-Papaya Chutney

Make this fresh chutney in late spring and summer when papayas are in season. Fresh chiles, lime, and fragrant spices make this very lively. This chutney goes well with marinated tofu or grilled vegetables.

3 cups cubed fresh pineapple (½-inch pieces)
1½ cups white vinegar
1 cup firmly packed brown sugar
1 medium onion, finely chopped
2 jalapeno peppers, finely chopped
2 cloves garlic, minced
½ cup finely chopped preserved ginger
½ cup seedless raisins
½ cup chopped papaya
½ fresh lime, peeled, seeded, and chopped
¼ cup chopped pitted dates
1 teaspoon cardamom
½ teaspoon salt
¼ teaspoon each ground cloves, ground allspice, and cayenne
¼ cup fresh lemon juice

Combine all ingredients except lemon juice in a heavy saucepan and bring to a boil. Reduce heat and simmer 1 hour, stirring frequently. Stir in lemon juice and simmer an additional 5 minutes. Cool completely before serving.

MAKES 1 QUART

Variation: Any fruit such as peaches, apricots, plums, mangos, or apples can be substituted for the pineapple and/or papaya.

Apricot Chutney

Fresh ginger and cayenne add just a hint of heat to this rich chutney. It makes a delicious sandwich with cream cheese.

1 pound dried apricots
10 cloves garlic
3 to 6 inches ginger
1¼ cups red wine vinegar, divided
2 cups white sugar
¼ teaspoon salt
¼ to ¾ teaspoon cayenne
½ cup currants
¾ cup golden raisins

Soak the apricots in 4 cups of boiling water for 1 hour. Cut into ¼-inch pieces or chop until chunky in a food processor; set aside. Blend garlic, ginger, and ¼ cup vinegar in a food processor. Mix apricots, ginger mixture, remaining vinegar, sugar, salt, and cayenne and bring to a boil. Simmer for 45 minutes to 1 hour; add currants and raisins and simmer gently until thick. Allow the chutney to sit for 1 or 2 hours before serving.

The chutney will keep in the refrigerator for a 1 to 2 weeks if stored in a tightly sealed container.

MAKES 3 CUPS

Date Chutney

This chutney is delicious with goat cheese or cream cheese.

1 cup pitted and chopped dried dates
1 tablespoon finely diced ginger
⅛ to ¼ teaspoon cayenne
½ teaspoon salt
4 tablespoons water
2 tablespoons chopped cilantro
juice of 1 lemon

Put all ingredients, except lemon juice, into a food processor and blend until smooth. Spoon into a bowl and add lemon juice, mixing thoroughly. Serve at room temperature.

MAKES 1 CUP

Spicy Peanut Sambal

This spicy, nutty sauce is good served with small salad-like dishes, fried tempeh, or raw vegetables. In Indonesia, this sambal is made in a mortar but you can use a blender or food processor instead, though it won't be the same consistency.

3 to 4 jalapenos, chopped
4 cloves garlic
¼ cup peanut butter
5 teaspoons soy sauce
4 teaspoons lime juice
4 teaspoons tamarind paste
4 teaspoons brown sugar
2 tablespoons water, or more

Put all ingredients into a blender and blend until smooth. If the sauce seems too thick, add water a teaspoon at a time to reach the desired consistency.

MAKES ½ CUP

Kamal's Sweet Tomato Chutney

This spicy-sweet chutney is great with goat cheese and roasted vegetables.

¼ teaspoon fenugreek
¼ teaspoon fennel
2 bay leaves
¼ teaspoon ground mace
¼ teaspoon garam marsala
3 medium-sized tomatoes (about ¾ pound total), finely chopped
10 cloves garlic, minced
1½ teaspoons grated ginger
¼ cup raisins
¼ teaspoon cayenne
2 cups white vinegar
1¼ teaspoons salt
2 cups sugar

Grind the first 5 ingredients together in a spice mill and set aside. Combine the tomatoes, garlic, ginger, raisins, cayenne, and spice mixture in a heavy skillet. Cook, uncovered, over medium-high heat, stirring occasionally, until most of the liquid is evaporated, about 12 minutes.

Add the vinegar, salt, and sugar and bring to a boil. Reduce the heat, cover, and simmer until thick, about 15 to 20 minutes. Spoon into clean jars and seal or refrigerate.

MAKES 2 CUPS

Sweet and Fragrant
Pineapple Chutney

What do you do with a pineapple that is too tart? Turn it into this delicious chutney.

1 average-sized, medium-ripe pineapple
1½ teaspoons ground cumin
1½ teaspoons ground fennel
¼ teaspoon cinnamon
¼ to ½ teaspoon cayenne
¼ to ½ teaspoon black pepper
juice of 1 lemon
1½ teaspoons coarse salt, or to taste
1½ cups sugar

Peel and core the pineapple. Put the pineapple into a food processor and process until coarsely pureed (or chop the pulp finely, using a sharp knife).

Put the pureed pineapple and all the other ingredients in a medium-sized pan over medium heat. Heat the mixture, stirring often, until the sugar completely dissolves and bring to a boil. Cook, uncovered, over low heat until the contents of the pan look thick and glazed like jam, about 30 minutes.

Turn off the heat, pour into sterilized jars, and seal. Although it is ready to serve, the flavor improves with 2 to 3 days of resting at room temperature. It will keep indefinitely until opened, then it needs to be refrigerated.

MAKES 4 CUPS

Peach Chutney

Make this chutney during the summer when peaches are sweet and plentiful. Serve over fresh soft cheeses with crackers as an appetizer or with savory spreads to add balance.

2 tablespoons oil
1 cup finely chopped onion
2 cloves garlic
10 ripe peaches, peeled and sliced
2 to 4 tablespoons cider vinegar
¼ cup honey

¼ teaspoon cinnamon
⅛ teaspoon nutmeg
⅛ teaspoon cardamom
⅛ teaspoon cayenne
1 teaspoon fresh grated ginger

Heat the oil and saute onion and garlic until golden brown. Add the peaches and cider vinegar and cook until the peaches begin to soften. Add the remaining ingredients and simmer until the sauce reaches a chunky consistency, about 30 minutes or so. Spoon into clean jars and seal or refrigerate up to 2 weeks.

MAKES 1 QUART

Mint Chutney

Mint, ginger and chiles give a vibrant flavor to sandwiches, or mix with yogurt and serve as a dip.

4 cups fresh mint leaves, packed
1 medium-sized onion, chopped
1 ounce fresh gingerroot, peeled and chopped
4 fresh green chiles
1 tablespoon fresh lemon juice
1½ tablespoons water
1½ tablespoons oil
sugar, to taste

In a blender, combine the mint leaves and all other ingredients. Blend to a fine paste. Store in covered container in refrigerator up to 1 week.

MAKES 1 CUP

"Empowering yourself to cook means giving yourself permission to try things out, to find things out. You allow your curiosity and enthusiasm some space to cavort, tasting and experimenting with unfamiliar (and familiar) ingredients. Although you may have a tentative plan or agenda, still you leave yourself space to follow your nose or play it by ear."

—EDWARD ESPE BROWN

Green Coconut Chutney

This chutney is unlike that of other chutneys in taste and texture. Try it with grilled vegetables, tofu, or curries.

1 lemon
1 to 2 fresh green chiles, seeded and chopped
½ cup chopped fresh mint or cilantro
2 scallions, chopped
1 teaspoon salt
1 cup shredded coconut
1 teaspoon oil
2 teaspoons black mustard seeds
2 teaspoons cumin seeds

Peel the lemon so the white pith remains, then cut into pieces and remove seeds.

Put into a blender or food processor with the chiles, mint, scallions, and salt and puree. Add coconut and continue blending until it forms a smooth paste, adding water if necessary.

Heat oil in a small pan and fry the mustard seeds until they pop, then add the cumin seeds. Add to the coconut paste and stir. Serve at room temperature. This chutney solidifies if chilled. Keeps refrigerated for 1 week.

MAKES 2 CUPS

Date-Coconut Chutney

This sweet and savory chutney adds exotic taste and texture to sandwiches.

4 ounces pitted dates, chopped
3 tablespoons shredded coconut
4 tablespoons fresh lemon juice
2 tablespoons grated ginger
½ teaspoon ground fennel seeds
½ teaspoon coriander
¼ cup chopped fresh parsley
½ teaspoon salt
¼ teaspoon cayenne (optional)

Mix together all ingredients and let sit for flavors to blend. If too thick, add lemon juice or water. Store tightly covered in the refrigerator. Keeps about 2 weeks.

MAKES 1 CUP

Peanut Chutney

Mako's words of wisdom: It is important that cilantro always be chopped before using in a food processor or blender to ensure even blending. Use this chutney as a condiment spread on sandwiches, with grilled tofu or vegetables, or with curries.

2 hot green chiles, seeded, deveined, and chopped
1 cup roasted peanuts
½ cup chopped cilantro
1 teaspoon coriander
1 tablespoon grated fresh ginger
½ cup yogurt
1 teaspoon sugar
½ teaspoon salt

Put ingredients together in a blender and blend until a fine but slightly coarse mixture forms. If necessary, let the mixture sit for an hour so that it softens, then resume blending into a soft paste. Serve at room temperature. Store in covered container in refrigerator up to 1 week.

MAKES 2 CUPS

Miso Sauce

This sauce is delicious with deep-fried eggplant and the Wa Fu Dressing (see page 128) for salads. It's a very adaptable sauce.

kombu or kombu/shiitake stock, rice vinegar, or sesame oil to thin to desired
   consistency
¼ cup mirin
⅓ cup sugar
¾ cup white miso

Heat the stock and whisk in the other ingredients (don't bring to a full boil for the sake of the miso). Can thicken with cornstarch. Store in a covered container in refrigerator.

MAKES ABOUT 1½ CUPS

Sweet Pepper Sauce

This roasted pepper and tomato sauce can be used as a compliment to polenta, pasta or roasted vegetables.

1½ pounds sweet bell peppers
2 tablespoons olive oil
1 cup chopped onion
¼ cup chopped celery with leaves
1 teaspoon minced garlic
1½ cups peeled, seeded, and minced tomatoes
½ teaspoon thyme
salt and pepper, to taste

Preheat oven to 400 degrees F. Place bell peppers on a lightly oiled baking pan and roast for 45 minutes, turning once or twice, until the skin is charred. Cut roasted peppers into ½-inch strips. Heat oil and saute onion and celery until wilted and golden. Add garlic and cook for 30 seconds. Stir in tomatoes, peppers, and thyme. Cover and simmer for 5 minutes. Uncover and simmer for 15 to 30 minutes (or until thickened, which depends on the juiciness of the tomatoes). Puree the mixture in a blender or food processor until smooth. Season with salt and pepper.

Cappon Magro Sauce

Try this sauce, from Deborah Madison's Vegetarian Cooking For Everyone, *over hot potatoes, beets, artichokes, hard-boiled eggs, or in pasta salad.*

1 thick slice white bread, crusts removed
2 tablespoons red wine vinegar
1 clove garlic, minced
2 tablespoons marjoram leaves
3 tablespoons capers, drained

½ cup pine nuts
1 cup finely minced parsley
2 tablespoons pitted green olives
⅓ to ½ cup extra virgin olive oil
salt and pepper, to taste

Soak the bread in vinegar. In a mortar and pestle, combine the garlic, marjoram, capers, pine nuts, parsley, and olives. Pound them until you have a coarse puree. Add the soaked bread and olive oil and grind some more. Season with salt and pepper and add a little more oil and/or vinegar if necessary to thin. The sauce should be thick, almost like a paste. Store in a covered container in refrigerator upto 1 week.

MAKES 2 CUPS

Romesco Sauce

This sauce is good over vegetables, roasted potatoes, or as a topping for sandwiches or crostini. The recipe is from Deborah Madison's Vegetarian Cooking For Everyone.

⅓ cup blanched almonds, or a mixture of hazelnuts and almonds
1 roasted red bell pepper, seeded and diced
3 cloves garlic
1 tablespoon chopped parsley
¼ teaspoon salt

1 teaspoon sweet paprika
½ teaspoon red pepper flakes
¼ cup red wine vinegar or sherry vinegar
½ cup extra virgin olive oil, preferably Spanish
salt and pepper, to taste

Toast the almonds until they are lightly browned. Finely chop them in a food processor, then add the remaining ingredients except the vinegar, oil, salt, and pepper and puree. Gradually pour in the vinegar, then the oil. Taste for salt and pepper. Store in a covered container in refrigerator up to 1 week.

MAKES 2 CUPS

Chermoula
(Moraccan Green Sauce)

This marinade for fish is also tasty with vegetables—especially sweet ones like beets, carrots, and winter squash. The recipe is from Deborah Madison's Vegetarian Cooking For Everyone.

4 cloves garlic, coarsely chopped

1 teaspoon salt
⅔ cup finely chopped cilantro
⅓ cup finely chopped parsley

1½ teaspoons sweet paprika
½ teaspoon cumin
⅛ teaspoon cayenne
¼ cup extra virgin olive oil
juice of 2 lemons

Pound the garlic with the salt in a mortar until smooth. Add the cilantro and parsley and pound a little more to bruise the leaves and release their flavor. Stir in the spices, olive oil, and lemon juice, to taste. Store in refrigerator up to 1 week.

MAKES 1½ CUPS

Yogurt Sauce
with Cayenne and Dill

Although simple, this sauce from Deborah Madison's Vegetarian Cooking For Everyone *is excellent spooned over grains, tossed with raw vegetables, or even stirred into lentils or spinach to make a quick salad. Since it's a condiment, use whole milk yogurt to give it body and texture.*

1 cup whole milk yogurt
½ cup sour cream
1 large clove garlic, minced
½ teaspoon salt

2 teaspoons chopped fresh dill
¼ teaspoon cayenne or hot paprika, or
  to taste

Whisk the yogurt and sour cream together. Mash the garlic with the salt in a mortar to a paste; measure 1 teaspoon, then add it to the yogurt with the dill and cayenne. Refrigerate for 1 hour to let the flavors to develop.

MAKES 1½ CUPS

Cha Cha Sauce

This peanut sauce is an adaptation of a peanut sambal used in Indonesian dishes. Try it with deep-fried strips of tempeh or tofu.

8 cloves garlic, mashed into a paste
2½ tablespoons grated gingerroot
¼ cup tamarind paste
¼ cup lime juice
¼ cup brown sugar
⅓ cup tamari
½ cup chunky peanut butter
cayenne pepper, to taste
salt and pepper, to taste
dry mustard to taste (optional)

Mix together all ingredients in a bowl. The hotness and blend of flavors depends on your personal preference as always. Leave some chunks of peanuts when blending for a nice texture. Add water to thin if necessary. Store in a covered container in refrigerator up to 2 weeks.

MAKES 2 CUPS

Pine Nut Sauce
with Lemon and Garlic

This tartar sauce uses pine nuts, but depending on where in the Middle East it's made, the nuts could be almonds, hazelnuts, or walnuts. It's excellent with cooked greens, grilled vegetables, and warm pita bread.

1 slice dense white bread, crusts removed
1 clove garlic
¼ teaspoon salt
½ cup pine nuts, toasted
½ to 1 cup water or vegetable stock
2 tablespoons fresh lemon juice
salt
chopped parsley
paprika or cayenne, to taste

Cover the bread with a little water and set aside to soak. In a mortar or food processor, grind the garlic, salt, and nuts. Squeeze the bread to remove the water. Add bread to the mix as well. Add water or stock until the sauce is smooth and thin, then season with lemon juice and taste for salt. The sauce will thicken as it sits so you may need to thin it out again with a little warm water. Pour into a bowl, sprinkle with a little chopped parsley and a dash of paprika or cayenne. Store in a covered container in refrigerator up to 1 week.

MAKES 2 CUPS

Salsa de Mancha Manteles

A mole-lover's salsa! Try this with crisp tortilla chips or compose an appetizer plate trio using this salsa, Black Bean Spread (see page 000), Mexican Tempeh Salad (see page 88), and fresh corn tortillas.

½ cup blanched, roasted almonds
3 tablespoons toasted sesame seeds
½ stick cinnamon
½ cup raisins
1 tablespoon vegetable oil (or sunflower, safflower, or soy)
1 clove garlic
2 cups dried red chiles, boiled and ground
1 ounce dark chocolate, chopped
sugar, to taste
salt, to taste

Place almonds, sesame seeds, cinnamon, and raisins into a food processor and blend to make a paste; set aside.

In a large pan, add oil and cook garlic until browned. Add the ground chiles and the almond mixture and cook until thickened. Add the chocolate and heat through until melted. Add the sugar and salt to taste. If the paste is very thick or spicy, try adding a little tomato paste. Store in refrigerator up to 2 weeks.

MAKES 2 CUPS

Salsa Verde with Walnuts and Tarragon

Everything in this sauce should be chopped fine—by hand for the best flavor and texture.

½ cup walnut pieces
2 small cloves garlic
1 cup Italian parsley (about 1 large bunch)
2 tablespoons tarragon
2 tablespoons capers, rinsed
1 cup extra virgin olive oil
1 teaspoon red wine vinegar, or to taste
salt and fresh-ground pepper, to taste

Combine the nuts, garlic, parsley, tarragon, and capers in a small bowl. Stir in the oil and vinegar, then season with salt and pepper to taste. Store in a jar in refrigerator.

MAKES 2 CUPS

Cilantro Salsa

Use this as a dip, in sandwiches in place of condiments, or with grilled vegetables.

1 jalapeno pepper
1 large bunch cilantro, stems removed
½ cup basil leaves
¼ cup mint leaves
2 cloves garlic, minced
juice from 1 or 2 limes
¼ cup water
½ cup plus 2 tablespoons olive oil
½ teaspoon cumin
½ teaspoon coriander
salt, to taste

Chop everything very finely, then stir in water, oil, and seasonings. Taste for salt and adjust the balance of lime juice to oil if needed. Store in a covered container in refrigerator up to 1 week.

MAKES 2 CUPS

marinades for tofu, tempeh & vegetables

"In the beginner's mind there are many possibilities,
but in the expert's there are few."

—SHUNRYU SUZUKI ROSHI

At Tassajara, the Bag Lunch Crew often uses an experimental approach to marinades. They try using different amounts of soy sauce, mushroom stir-fry sauce, mirin, sake, rice vinegar, and sesame oil in combination with pickled ginger, minced fresh ginger, minced garlic, chili flakes, red onion slices, red pepper slices, scallions, basil, peanut butter (thinned with water), and tahini (thinned with water).

They also went for an Italian approach with olive oil mixed with equal parts of balsamic vinegar and soy sauce in combination with fresh herbs such as rosemary, oregano, basil, thyme, sage, and savory.

For marinating tofu, simply cut each block into ⅓-inch-thick slices or for triangles, cut each slice again diagonally to make a triangle. (A block of tofu could be anywhere from 4 to 6 ounces depending on the brand.) The marinade is then poured over the tofu and baked for 20 to 30 minutes at 350 degrees F.

If pressed tofu is needed, place the tofu on a pie plate and top with a second plate. Weight the plate with a heavy pan and press for at least 30 minutes. If the tofu used was fresh and fairly dry when marinated, the marinade can be boiled, strained, and kept refrigerated for reuse.

Although some recipes call for marinating the tofu for hours or overnight, Deborah Madison (*Green's Cookbook*), says that another effective use of a marinade is to use it as a cooking liquid. Simply pour the marinade over the tofu as it cooks. Try it either way.

The marinades listed for tofu can also be used for vegetables. For vegetables such as zucchini, squash, and eggplant, cut them into ¼- to ⅓-inch-thick slices, dip into bowls of marinade and place on an oiled sheet pan. Leave the portobello and shiitake mushrooms whole so they retain their juices. Bake for 15 to 20 minutes at 375 degrees F. Turn over and bake another 15 to 20 minutes, or until tender but still retaining their texture. For deeper flavors, marinate the vegetables for up to 2 hours, then cook as desired.

Suggested vegetables that lend themselves well to marinating are red and green bell peppers, summer squashes, new potatoes, onions, fennel, mushrooms, southwestern peppers, and eggplant. Try roasting, grilling, or baking after marinating. At Tassajara, the marinated vegetables are baked or roasted when used for the Bag Lunch.

Sesame Marinade

Sesame Marinade

This recipe is from Vegetarian Cooking for Everyone *by Deborah Madison. This marinade makes an excellent sauce for grilled eggplant and Chinese noodles as well as tofu.*

2 tablespoons light sesame oil

1 tablespoon dark sesame oil

¼ cup soy sauce

5 teaspoons balsamic or rice wine
   vinegar

1½ tablespoons sugar, or to taste

½ teaspoon red pepper flakes

2 tablespoons chopped scallions

1½ tablespoons chopped cilantro

Combine all ingredients together in a bowl and stir until the sugar is dissolved. Taste and adjust for sweetness if needed. Depending on the type of soy sauce you've used, you may need to add more sugar for balance.

MAKES 1 CUP

Orange-Balsamic Marinated Tofu

This citrus-flavored marinade goes particularly well with fresh basil. Use any leftover mari-nade to dress a salad made of mixed greens, sliced oranges and slivered almonds.

12 ounces firm tofu

3 tablespoons fresh lemon juice

3 tablespoons fresh orange juice

⅔ cup balsamic vinegar

4 cloves garlic, minced

1 teaspoon salt

1 cup olive oil

fresh basil, chopped, to taste (optional)

Slice the block of tofu into thirds and then cut each third into slices. Combine all ingredi-ents except tofu in a bowl and mix well; adjust seasonings. Pour marinade over tofu and let sit for at least 2 hours or longer in the refrigerator. Remove tofu from marinade and put on a slanted surface, usually a cutting board or baking tray to drain; drain for 20 minutes. It is now ready to grill, bake, or fry.

MAKES ABOUT 1½ CUPS

The Tassajara Marinated Tofu

This marinade is from The Tassajara Recipe Book *by Edward Espe Brown. This is a strong marinade, very rich in earthy flavors. If using tofu, be sure to cut it into about ½-inch slices in order for it to absorb the marinade. This is the main marinade Tassajara uses to make brochettes—marinated tofu and vegetables on skewers for grilling or on the barbecue.*

> 2 (12-ounce) blocks firm tofu
> ½ ounce dried mushrooms
> 1 cup water
> 2 teaspoons dried oregano
> 2 cloves garlic, minced
> ½ cup fruity olive oil
> ½ cup sherry wine vinegar or red wine vinegar
> ½ cup red wine
> ½ cup soy sauce (tamari if possible)
> pinch of ground cloves
> ½ teaspoon salt
> fresh-ground black pepper

Drain and press the tofu (as explained on page 115) to remove excess water.

In a saucepan, simmer the mushrooms in water for 15 minutes. Toast the oregano in a small frying pan over medium heat until it becomes aromatic (without burning).

Combine all ingredients except tofu. Bring to a boil and simmer about 3 to 4 minutes more.

Cut the tofu into 4 slices and place in a baking dish. Pour the hot marinade over the tofu. Marinate in the refrigerator for at least 2 hours, preferably overnight. The tofu can marinate several days. Grill, bake, or broil tofu or vegetables as desired.

MAKES ABOUT 3 CUPS

Judith's Marinade

The addition of mirin gives this marinade a subtle sweetness.

1 cup tamari
⅔ cup mirin
2 cloves garlic, minced

⅓ cup sesame oil
2 teaspoons dry mustard
¾ cup water

Combine all ingredients in a small bowl. Can use to marinate vegetables or tofu.

MAKES 3 CUPS

Tofu Teriyaki

This recipe is also from The Tassajara Recipe Cookbook *by Edward Espe Brown. This dish is fairly juicy, so it's excellent served over plain rice or noodles.*

2 (12-ounce) blocks firm tofu
1 cup soy sauce
½ cup sake or white wine
½ cup sugar (or part honey)

1 tablespoon grated fresh ginger
6 cloves garlic, minced
¼ cup sesame oil
1½ teaspoons dry mustard

Cut the tofu blocks in half and press as described on page 115 if necessary. Cut the tofu in approximately 1 x 1 x 2-inch-thick slices.

Meanwhile, combine the rest of the ingredients in a saucepan and heat to boiling; simmer for 10 minutes. Pour the hot marinade over the tofu and let marinate a few hours or overnight, if desired. Bake tofu, uncovered, at 350 degrees F for about 45 minutes, or until heated through. You can also saute onions, bell peppers and mushrooms for about 2 minutes, layer with tofu, and then bake as directed above.

MAKES ABOUT 3 CUPS

Tofu Marinated
with Parsley and Olive Oil

This tofu is a little unusual, as the tofu is not cooked after marinating. It has a fresh, herb and garlic taste. It can be grilled or, if preferred, it can be baked at 350 degrees F for about 40 minutes.

2 (12-ounce) blocks firm tofu
3 cloves garlic, minced
1 cup finely chopped parsley
½ teaspoon salt
pinch black pepper
3 tablespoons capers
⅓ cup fresh lemon juice
fresh herbs such as basil, oregano, or thyme (optional)
⅓ cup olive oil

Slice blocks of tofu into thirds and then each third into slices, then into cubes. Mix garlic, parsley, salt, pepper, capers, lemon juice, and fresh herbs, if using, in a small mixing bowl. Let stand for a few minutes, and then pour in the olive oil; stir to combine. Coat each piece of tofu with the mixture and then layer in shallow sheet pan. Let stand overnight and serve on platters with a garnish of fresh herbs. Serve at room temperature.

MAKES ABOUT 3 CUPS

Honey-Mustard Tofu

This is the most requested tofu recipe for the Bag Lunch at Tassajara.

½ cup fresh lemon juice
¼ cup olive or other vegetable oil
2 tablespoons honey
¼ cup Dijon mustard
salt and fresh-ground pepper, to taste
1 (12-ounce) package firm tofu

Preheat oven to 350 degrees F. Whisk the lemon juice, oil, honey, and mustard in a small bowl; add salt and pepper and then set aside.

Drain and press tofu if necessary. Cut block of tofu into thirds and then each third into triangles. Place in a 9 x 13-inch baking pan and pour the marinade over top, making sure to completely cover. Let tofu marinate for at least 2 hours and then bake for 20 to 30 minutes, or until crispy but still moist inside.

MAKES **6** TRIANGLES

Hoisin Marinade

This is a classic hoisin marinade, delicious for barbecued tofu.

¼ cup hoisin sauce
¼ cup mirin
2½ tablespoons soy sauce
1½ tablespoons brown sugar
1½ tablespoons ketchup
3 cloves garlic, minced

Combine all ingredients in a bowl and blend well.

MAKES 1 CUP

"So the secret is to just say 'Yes!' and jump off from here. Then there is no problem. It means to be yourself, always yourself, without sticking to an old self."

—SHUNRYU SUZUKI ROSHI

salads, dressings, pickles & relishes

Couscous Salad

The flavors of Dijon mustard and coriander add zing to this delicious grain salad. A perfect addition to any picnic.

1⅓ cups water
1 cup couscous
½ teaspoon salt
⅓ cup olive oil
¼ cup lemon juice
2 cloves garlic, minced
1½ teaspoons Dijon mustard
1½ teaspoons ground coriander
fresh-ground black pepper, to taste
1 cup cooked garbanzo beans
½ cup chopped green onions
1 cup chopped tomato
½ cup seeded and chopped cucumber
½ cup minced parsley

In a small saucepan, bring the water to a boil and add the couscous and salt. Remove the pan from the heat, cover, and let sit 5 minutes. Just before using, fluff with a fork.

To make the dressing, whisk together the olive oil, lemon juice, garlic, Dijon, coriander, and pepper in a small bowl.

In a large bowl, combine the couscous, garbanzo beans, green onions, tomato, cucumber and parsley; mix well. Add the dressing and toss to combine. Chill for at least 2 hours before serving to allow the flavors to develop.

MAKES ABOUT 4 CUPS

Edamame Salad

This is a delicious way to incorporate fresh, high-protein edamame into your diet. Serve it as a side to Tofu Teriyaki (see page 123).

¾ ounce dried arame (seaweed)
3 tablespoons rice vinegar
3 tablespoons soy sauce
2 tablespoons sesame oil
1 teaspoon sugar
1 tablespoon sesame seeds
1 red bell pepper, cut into thin slices
1 green bell pepper, cut into thin slices
1 cup fresh edemame, cooked
16 ounces soba noodles, cooked

Soak the seaweed in warm water to cover for 5 minutes. Drain and then squeeze out excess water.

Stir together the rice vinegar, soy sauce, sesame oil, and sugar in a bowl until well dissolved. Combine the sesame seeds, bell peppers, edamame, and noodles and then toss with dressing. Serve cold.

MAKES 1½ QUARTS

VARIATION: *Instead of using soba noodles, increase edamame noodles to 16 ounces and make it a marinated vegetable salad.*

Cabbage Shanghai Salad

This is a delicious, light salad. Try using it as a complement to Asian meals.

2 cups hot water
4 cups shredded nappa cabbage
2 cloves garlic, minced
1 teaspoon ginger
2 tablespoons black sesame seeds
½ cup rice vinegar
2 tablespoons sesame oil
2 tablespoons honey
salt, to taste

Just before serving, pour hot water over cabbage, cover and let sit to wilt, about 10 minutes; drain. Combine remaining ingredients in a separate bowl and then toss with cabbage.

MAKES 1½ QUARTS

Eggplant and Red Pepper Salad

This salad makes a wonderful addition to antipasto platters with Tuscan White Bean Salad (see page 137), hard-boiled eggs, and olives.

1 pound Japanese eggplant, ¼-inch diagonal slices
2 tablespoons olive oil
3 cloves garlic, minced
salt and fresh-ground pepper, to taste
1 red bell pepper, cut into matchsticks
¼ cup thinly sliced shallots
2 tablespoons pine nuts, lightly toasted
balsamic vinegar, to taste

Toss eggplant with olive oil, garlic, salt, and pepper. Bake at 400 degrees F for 15 to 20 minutes, or until just barely done. Combine eggplant, bell pepper, shallots, and pine nuts (reserve a few for the garnish) in a small bowl. Add balsamic vinegar to taste. Garnish with reserved nuts.

MAKES 4 CUPS

Peperonata

Try this summer dish from Deborah Madison's Vegetarian Cooking For Everyone *when tomatoes and peppers abound. Serve it with bruschetta, pasta, or composed salad plates.*

2 tablespoons olive oil
1 onion, diced
2 cloves garlic, thinly sliced
1 bay leaf
½ teaspoon minced fresh thyme
1 each red, yellow, and green bell pepper, diced or sliced
¼ teaspoon salt
3 ripe tomatoes, peeled, seeded, and diced
pepper, to taste

Heat the olive oil in a wide skillet. Add the onion, garlic, bay leaf, and thyme. Cook over medium-high heat, stirring frequently, until the onions are soft and lightly colored, about 10 minutes. Add the peppers, season with salt, and raise the heat. Cook briskly until the peppers begin to soften, then add the tomatoes and reduce the heat to medium. Simmer, stirring occasionally, until the excess water from the tomato has cooked away, about 15 minutes. Discard bay leaf. Taste for salt and season with pepper.

MAKES 4 CUPS

Green Rice Salad

This salad gets its vibrant green color from fresh herbs. Serve at picnics or barbecues with tofu and vegetable brochettes.

BALSAMIC VINAIGRETTE
- ¼ cup olive oil
- 1 tablespoon balsamic vinegar
- 2 teaspoons fresh lemon juice
- 1½ tablespoons minced green onions
- 1 tablespoon minced parsley
- 2 to 3 cloves garlic, minced
- ¼ teaspoon sugar
- salt and pepper, to taste

- 1 cup cooked long-grain brown rice
- 1 cup cooked long-grain white rice
- ½ cup finely chopped green onions
- 1 to 1½ cups fresh herbs, minced (parsley, cilantro, oregano, tarragon, or thyme)
- ½ cup grated white cheddar or asiago cheese
- 1 cup frozen peas, thawed
- ⅓ cup pine nuts
- shredded lettuce
- sprig of fresh herbs

Combine all the vinaigrette ingredients together. Toss with the warm rice and then let cool. Toss with onions, herbs, cheese, peas, and nuts. Serve on shredded lettuce, and garnish with fresh herbs.

MAKES 1½ QUARTS

Mango Pepper Salad

This is a delightful and refreshing salad. Serve it in hollowed-out vegetables as a salad or appetizer, or compose a lunch plate with this and Garlic, Cilantro, and Chipotle Hummus (see page 61).

3 mangos, cut into ¾-inch cubes
2 green bell peppers, julienned
½ red onion, sliced, then cut slices in half to create moons
2 tablespoons chopped mint
¼ cup wine vinegar
2 tablespoons brown sugar
1 tablespoon olive oil
salt and fresh-ground pepper, to taste
cilantro, for garnish

Combine all ingredients in a bowl and let sit about 30 minutes before serving.

MAKES 1½ QUARTS

Tuscan White Bean Salad

This recipe is great with Eggplant and Red Pepper Salad (see page 133), hard-boiled eggs, and olives on antipasto plates. You can also add diced red bell peppers and/or carrots.

2 whole cloves
2 bay leaves
several sprigs fresh thyme
several fresh sage leaves
few black peppercorns
1½ cups dried small white beans, soaked overnight
2 to 3 cloves garlic, minced
½ teaspoon salt
1½ to 2 teaspoons Dijon mustard
3 tablespoons sherry wine vinegar
⅔ cup olive oil
1 small red onion, diced
½ cup diced celery
1 tablespoon each minced summer savory or fresh oregano and Italian parsley
6 to 8 kalamata olives, finely chopped
salt and fresh-ground black pepper, to taste

Tie the cloves, bay leaves, thyme, sage, and peppercorns into a piece of cheesecloth or put into a tea ball. Simmer the beans with the herbs in 2 quarts water until tender and soft, but still hold their shape, about 1 hour; drain and remove herbs.

Pound the garlic and salt into a paste and combine with the mustard and vinegar. Whisk in the olive oil and taste for seasoning. While the beans are still warm, gently toss with the vinaigrette and remaining ingredients; adjust seasonings. Garnish with olives and herbs. For deeper flavor, allow the salad to marinate before serving.

MAKES 2 QUARTS

Indonesian Salad
with Peanut Dressing

This salad is definitely worth the effort. The rich peanut dressing is the perfect complement to fresh, crunchy vegetables and tofu.

1 tablespoon peanut oil

16 ounces firm tofu, cut into 1-inch cubes

6 cups mixed baby salad greens

1 cup French green beans or sugar snap peas, lightly blanched

1 carrot, peeled and julienned

2 medium tomatoes, cut into 4 wedges each

1 cup mung bean sprouts

1 small cucumber, peeled, seeded, and sliced into moons

¼ cup cilantro leaves

PEANUT DRESSING

½ cup firm silken tofu

3 tablespoons peanut butter

2 tablespoons soy sauce

5 tablespoons rice vinegar

2 tablespoons maple syrup

1 tablespoon sugar

1 tablespoon grated ginger

¼ teaspoon red chili flakes

4 tablespoons light coconut milk

1 scallion, finely chopped

Heat oil in a small skillet and cook tofu cubes until lightly browned. Drain on paper towels and set aside. On a large platter, arrange salad greens, green beans, carrot, tomatoes, sprouts, and cucumber. Sprinkle with tofu cubes.

For the dressing, combine all ingredients in a blender and blend until smooth and creamy. Pour dressing over salad and serve garnished with cilantro leaves.

MAKES 1½ QUARTS

"Enter into your own body. There you'll find a
solid place to put your feet."

—KABIR

Cabbage Salad with Miso "Floating Cloud" Dressing

The Miso Floating Cloud Dressing is very popular at Tassajara and is what sets this cabbage salad apart. It is also good with a salad made of cabbage, tomatoes, and tofu.

⅔ cup vegetable oil (or safflower, sunflower, or soy)
1 teaspoon sesame oil
¼ cup lemon juice or rice vinegar
¼ cup red miso
1 clove garlic, minced
¼ teaspoon each powdered ginger and dry mustard, or to taste
4 cups shredded green cabbage
1 red bell pepper, julienned
1 red onion, julienned
½ cup toasted walnuts

Whisk together in a bowl the oils, lemon juice or vinegar, miso, garlic, ginger, and mustard.

Toss the cabbage, bell pepper, onion, and nuts in a medium-sized bowl. Pour dressing over top and mix well. Serve.

MAKES 1½ QUARTS

Japanese Marinated Salad
with Diced Tofu

This salad can also be used as a sandwich filling if drained well before using.

2 tablespoons soy sauce

3 tablespoons sesame oil

1 tablespoon rice vinegar

½ teaspoon sugar

12 ounces extra-firm tofu, pressed and cut into ½-inch cubes

1 cucumber, peeled, seeded, and diced

1 small carrot, diced

1 tomato, chopped fine

10 green beans, blanched and chopped fine

Whisk together the soy sauce, oil, vinegar, and sugar in a small bowl. Then combine the tofu and vegetables in a large bowl. Add dressing, cover bowl, and marinate for 8 to 10 hours in the refrigerator. Drain the vegetables slightly before serving.

MAKES 2 CUPS

Tabbouli Salad

This is a traditional Tabbouli salad, but here currants embellish the recipe.

1 cup bulgur	salt and fresh pepper
2¼ cups boiling water	3 tablespoons fresh lemon juice
1 cup minced green onions	½ cup chopped mint
1 cup minced parsley	4 tablespoons olive oil
1 tomato, chopped	¼ cup currants (optional)

Put the bulgur into a medium bowl and cover with boiling water. Cover the bowl with a plate and let sit for 20 minutes; drain with a fine mesh strainer.

Add the green onions, parsley, tomato, salt, and pepper and mix well; add lemon juice and then refrigerate. Just before serving, add mint, olive oil, and currants, if desired, and toss well. Serve in a bowl lined with lettuce leaves.

MAKES ABOUT 5 CUPS

Tassajara Bean Salad

This is Tassajara's version of the traditional bean salad recipe. The Balsamic Vinaigrette goes particularly well with beans. Canned beans can also be used, but be sure to rinse well before using.

½ cup dried black beans, cleaned, rinsed, and soaked, or 1 cup canned
½ cup dried white beans, cleaned, rinsed, and soaked, or 1 cup canned
½ cup dried pink beans, cleaned, rinsed, and soaked, or 1 cup canned
1 cup fresh green beans, slice into ½-inch diagonals
¼ cup sliced black olives
1 each red and green bell pepper, diced
½ cup diced celery
½ cup diced water chestnuts
fresh herbs, to taste (oregano, parsley, rosemary, thyme)

BALSAMIC VINAIGRETTE
⅓ cup balsamic vinegar
2½ tablespoons red wine vinegar
2 shallots, minced
salt and pepper, to taste
1¼ cups extra virgin olive oil

Cook the dried beans separately. Drain the beans, cover them with 6 cups fresh water and then bring to a boil. Boil, uncovered, for 10 minutes; skim off any foam. Lower the heat, cover, and simmer until the beans are tender, about 1 hour. If using canned beans, skip this step but rinse the beans well.

To make the vinaigrette, combine vinegars, shallots, and salt and pepper; whisk in the olive oil and taste for balance. While the beans are still warm, gently combine the beans with the vinaigrette; set aside.

Drop green beans into boiling water for 1 minute, remove, drain and rinse in cold water; set aside.

Combine the beans, green beans, and remaining ingredients. Toss with the vinaigrette and serve.

MAKES 1½ QUARTS

"This is the secret of the teaching. It may be so, but it is not always so. Without being caught by words or rules, without many preconceived ideas, we actually do something, and doing something, we apply our teaching."

—SHUNRYU SUZUKI ROSHI

Wa Fu Dressing

Try this dressing with a salad of wakame, carrots, daikon, cucumbers, radishes, and cherry tomatoes. Dress generously.

½ cup tamari
¼ cup sugar
¾ cup rice vinegar
1 tablespoon sesame oil
1 tablespoon toasted sesame seeds

Combine all ingredients in a bowl and mix well. Chill before using.

Lime Ume Dressing

This dressing is great with daikon or carrot-based salads. Soak them briefly, then drain well. Garnish with slivered nori.

½ cup lime juice
1½ tablespoons ume plum paste (umeboshi)
½ cup sugar
salt, to taste (this brings out the crucial flavor of the ume—otherwise it is too sweet/tart)

Combine all ingredients in a small bowl and whisk well to blend. Serve chilled.

Avocado Dressing

Serve on cabbage salads with fruit or vegetables. This dressing will keep its clear green color for several days in the refrigerator.

    1 medium-sized ripe avocado, peeled and pitted
    1 small onion, chopped
    ½ cup sour cream
    2 tablespoons lemon juice
    pinch of black pepper
    dash of Tabasco
    1 teaspoon salt

In a food processor, combine avocado and onion and blend until smooth. Combine in a small bowl with sour cream, lemon juice, pepper, Tabasco, and salt. Beat until smooth.

Poppy Seed Dressing

This dressing is a favorite for salads with fruit and greens.

    ½ cup honey
    6 tablespoons cider vinegar
    5 tablespoons olive oil
    2 small shallots, minced
    4 teaspoons Dijon mustard
    2 teaspoons poppy seeds
    salt and fresh-ground pepper, to taste

Whisk all ingredients together in a small bowl.

North African Lemon Dressing

This dressing is suggested for salads with tomatoes, sweet onions, cucumbers, green peppers, or fruit salads and cottage cheese. At Tassajara, we use it often with salads of lettuce and grape-fruit sections. A delicious variation can be made by using limes in place of lemons.

zest of 2 lemons
¼ cup lemon juice
1½ teaspoons salt
⅛ teaspoon cayenne or Tabasco sauce
2 cloves garlic, minced
⅔ to ¾ cup olive oil
½ teaspoon coriander
½ teaspoon cumin
½ teaspoon dry mustard
½ teaspoon paprika
1 teaspoon sugar

Combine all ingredients in a bowl; mix well and chill before serving.

Mustard Vinaigrette

Serve this vinaigrette with mixed greens or over fresh tomato slices.

¼ teaspoon tarragon
¼ teaspoon fennel seed, ground
2 tablespoons sherry vinegar
¼ teaspoon salt
2 tablespoons Dijon mustard
3 tablespoons melted butter
½ cup olive oil

Combine tarragon, fennel, vinegar, salt, and mustard in a small bowl. Whisk in butter and olive oil. Taste and adjust seasonings.

Marinated Mozzarella

Bocconcini, bite-sized balls of fresh mozzarella, makes a very attractive appetizer with this marinade.

⅓ cup balsamic vinegar
3 cloves garlic, minced
3 tablespoons Dijon mustard
3 tablespoons minced mixed fresh herbs (parsley, thyme, or marjoram)
2 cups olive oil
1 pound bocconcini

Combine all ingredients in a bowl and mix well. Let stand at least 1 hour garnished with fresh herbs.

MAKES 2 CUPS

VARIATION: *Balsamic vinegar is quite strong and dark. For a lighter version, use sherry wine vinegar or red wine vinegar.*

Antipasto Agrodolce
(Sweet and Sour Vegetables)

Try this Italian appetizer as part of an antipasto dish with fresh mozzarella, olives, and sliced baguettes.

2 bulbs garlic
2 tablespoons olive oil
2 sprigs fresh rosemary or thyme
2 red or yellow bell peppers, roasted and cut into ½-inch strips
2 red onions, quartered
½ cup plus 2 tablespoons balsamic vinegar
1 tablespoon butter
1 pound Japanese eggplant, cut into ¼-inch diagonals
salt and pepper, to taste

Preheat oven to 350 degrees F. The garlic, peppers, and onions can be roasted in the oven at the same time but note varying cooking times. Cut off the stem ends of the garlic and place cut side down in a small baking dish. Coat with olive oil and top with fresh herbs. Cover and roast until just tender, about 1 hour. When cool, squeeze cloves out of husks; set aside. To roast the peppers, place in a baking dish and roast for 30 to 40 minutes or so. When done, place the peppers in a paper bag and let sit a few minutes. Remove skins and seeds and then cut into ½-inch strips. To roast the onions, place in a baking dish and drizzle with 2 tablespoons balsamic vinegar, butter, and enough water to cover, toss gently. Roast for 30 minutes until tender but firm.

Meanwhile, heat ½ cup balsamic vinegar until it is has a slightly syrupy consistency. After the garlic is roasted, toss the eggplants with half of the garlic, salt, and pepper and brush with the reduced balsamic vinegar. Bake, uncovered, for 15 to 20 minutes, or until just tender. Dress the pepper strips with balsamic vinegar, the remaining half of the roasted garlic, salt, and pepper. Arrange the vegetables on a platter and garnish with roasted garlic if desired.

MAKES 2 QUARTS

Daikon Ginger Pickles

These are sweet pickles. Keep in mind if you use brown sugar, the pickles will be somewhat brown. Serve with the Tassajara Marinated Tofu (see page 125) or with sandwiches to add flavor and texture to the meal.

1 cup water
½ teaspoon salt
½ cup fresh ginger, cut into ¹⁄₁₆-inch slices
½ cup rice vinegar
5 tablespoons brown or white sugar
1¾ cups mirin
3 cups daikon, cut into ¹⁄₁₆-inch slices

Bring water and salt to a boil. Blanch ginger in water for 30 seconds; drain and set aside. In same pan, heat rice vinegar, sugar, and mirin until dissolved.

Slice daikon into slices, if too large, cut in halves or quarters to make bite-sized pieces. Put daikon and liquid mixture into a plastic container and cover; stir once a day. Pickles are ready in 5 days and keep for up to 1 month refrigerated.

MAKES 3 CUPS

Mama Sawyer's Cucumber Relish

These are sweet cucumber pickles and go well with savory marinated tofu or when a little something sweet is needed to complete a composed salad plate.

3 large cucumbers, peeled
1 large onion, peeled
½ teaspoon salt
1 cup white vinegar
1 cup sugar
3 tablespoons flour
1 teaspoon celery seed
1 teaspoon yellow mustard seed
4 teaspoons tumeric

Dice the cucumbers and onion into ½-inch pieces, add salt and let sit overnight; drain.

In a medium saucepan, combine the cucumber mixture with the remaining ingredients and then boil for 5 minutes.

MAKES 4 CUPS

Pungent Cucumbers

Serve these pickles alongside Asian-inspired themes such as Tofu Teriyaki, Edamame Salad and Sesame Cookies. Or simply serve inside of sandwiches and rollups.

4 large cucumbers, peeled, seeded, and sliced into ¼-inch half moons
½ cup bell peppers, cut into ⅛ x 2-inch strips
1 quart boiling water
¼ cup sugar
½ cup red wine vinegar
3 tablespoons grated ginger
2 tablespoons minced serrano chile pepper
2 tablespoons soy sauce
¼ cup sesame oil
2 dried red chiles
¼ cup Szechwan peppercorns

Mix cucumbers with bell peppers and place in a colander. Pour 1 quart boiling water over vegetables and let drain. Mix sugar, vinegar, ginger, serrano chiles, and soy sauce in a small saucepan and heat until the sugar dissolves.

In a separate skillet, heat oil, and add dried chiles and peppercorns. When the chiles have turned dark red, remove from heat and strain the oil into the sugar mixture. Mix with the cucumber mixture and let marinate for 2 to 6 hours. Serve cold.

MAKES 4 CUPS

Pickled Red Onions

These onion pickles go particularly well with Southwestern food. They are delicious with marinated black beans or rice salad. The recipe is from Deborah Madison's The Savory Way.

2 medium red onions, peeled and sliced into ¼-inch-thick rounds
1 quart boiling water
⅔ cup rice wine or champagne vinegar
⅔ cup water
pinch of sugar
pinch of hot pepper flakes
½ teaspoon black peppercorns

Place the onion rounds into a colander inside a bowl. Cover with boiling water and let sit for 3 to 5 minutes, or until the onions begin to soften and lose their sharp taste; drain and cover with vinegar and water. Add a pinch of sugar to cut the acidity and sprinkle with hot pepper flakes and black peppercorns. Cover and refrigerate until cool. These hold well, so make them in advance of serving.

MAKES 2 CUPS

Mushrooms a la Greque

This rich mushroom appetizer is good served with other marinated vegetables such as beets, or part of an antipasto platter.

MARINADE
¼ cup olive oil
½ cup corn oil
¼ cup red wine vinegar
1 bay leaf
1 teaspoon chervil
½ teaspoon oregano
1 tablespoon parsley
1 tablespoon dry mustard
1 teaspoon salt
¼ teaspoon fresh-ground pepper
1 pound mushrooms
¼ cup dry red wine

Bring all the marinade ingredients to a boil in a large pot, boil about 5 minutes. Add mushrooms; stir until they are moistened. Cover and cook another 5 minutes. Let the mushrooms cool; add the red wine. If desired, you can also drain the mushroom mixture before adding the wine.

MAKES 4 CUPS

dairy cookies

Chocolate Chews

Edward Brown says this isn't his recipe but everyone at the Zen Center believes it is. . . . These cookies are probably the most popular cookie ever served at Tassajara.

½ pound semisweet chocolate
3 ounces unsweetened chocolate
½ cup butter
¾ teaspoon instant coffee
3 eggs
1 cup brown sugar
1 cup unbleached flour
½ teaspoon baking powder
¼ teaspoon salt
2 teaspoons vanilla extract
1½ cups chocolate chips

Preheat oven to 325 degrees F. In a double boiler, melt the semisweet and unsweetened chocolate, butter, and coffee together.

Meanwhile, beat the eggs and brown sugar together until light in color and thick. Sift together the flour, baking powder, and salt.

Let the chocolate mixture cool slightly and then whisk into the eggs and sugar. Stir in the vanilla extract and then gently fold in the dry ingredients. Stir in the chocolate chips.

Drop by tablespoon onto a greased cookie sheet and bake for 12 to 15 minutes. Cool on a wire rack.

MAKES ABOUT 4 DOZEN COOKIES

Sonia's Shortbread Cookies

These non-traditional, but delicious, shortbread cookies use nuts to replace part of the wheat flour, and confectioners' sugar and oil to make the cookies light and fluffy.

1 cup butter (or use ½ cup butter and ½ cup vegetable oil)
½ cup confectioners' sugar
2 cups unbleached flour
2 cups ground nuts (almonds, walnuts, and/or pecans)
1 teaspoon baking powder

Preheat oven to 325 degrees F. Cream the butter and sugar together until light and fluffy. In another bowl, combine the flour, nuts, and baking powder; add to the butter mixture.

Drop by tablespoons onto a greased cookie sheet and bake for 12 to 15 minutes. Cool on a wire rack.

MAKES ABOUT 3 DOZEN COOKIES

Gingersnaps

This is a traditional gingersnap recipe but uses rich Blackstrap molasses to deepen the flavor of the cookies.

½ cup butter, at room temperature
¾ cup brown sugar
2 teaspoons Blackstrap molasses
1 egg
1½ tablespoons powdered ginger (double if using fresh)
2 teaspoons cinnamon
¼ teaspoon salt
½ teaspoon baking soda
½ teaspoon baking powder
1½ cups unbleached flour
½ cup white sugar

Preheat oven to 350 degrees F. Cream the butter, brown sugar, and molasses together and beat well. Add egg and beat until smooth.

In another bowl, stir together the ginger, cinnamon, salt, baking soda, baking powder, and flour. Gradually add to the butter mixture, blending thoroughly.

Roll the dough into balls about 1 inch in diameter. Coat each ball by rolling in the sugar. Flatten each ball with the bottom of a glass. Bake cookies on a greased cookie sheet for about 15 minutes, or until nicely browned. Cool on a wire rack.

VARIATIONS: *To bring out the ginger flavor, add some mustard powder and a pinch of cayenne or black pepper. Also, feel free to mix dry and fresh ginger and add diced pieces of candied ginger. Doubling the molasses is also good.*

MAKES ABOUT 1 DOZEN COOKIES

Pineapple-Coconut Bars

Transport yourself to the islands with these tropical-tasting cookie bars. They are the next best thing to being on a beach under a palm tree.

½ cup butter, at room temperature
1 cup firmly packed brown sugar
2 eggs
¼ teaspoon almond extract
¾ cup unbleached flour
¾ teaspoon baking powder
½ teaspoon salt
¾ cup flaked coconut
1 (8-ounce) can crushed pineapple, drained well

In a large bowl, beat butter and sugar together until creamy; beat in eggs and almond extract. In another bowl, stir together flour, baking powder, and salt; gradually add to butter mixture, blending thoroughly. Stir in coconut and pineapple.

Spread mixture evenly in a greased and floured 9-inch-square baking pan. Bake at 350 degrees F for 25 to 30 minutes, or until the top springs back when lightly touched. Let cool in pan on a wire rack, then cut into 1 x 2 ¼-inch bars.

MAKES 3 DOZEN BARS

Sesame Cookies

These sesame cookies have a rich and buttery taste and are a favorite of children.

⅔ cup canola oil or other vegetable oil
1 cup brown sugar
1 egg
1 teaspoon vanilla
1 teaspoon lemon zest
1 cup toasted sesame seeds
1 cup toasted coconut
2 cups unbleached flour
1 teaspoon baking powder
½ teaspoon baking soda
¾ teaspoon salt

Beat the oil, brown sugar, egg, vanilla, and lemon zest together. Stir in the sesame seeds and coconut.

In another bowl, stir together the flour, baking powder, baking soda, and salt; add to the sugar mixture and mix until combined. Do not overwork the dough or the cookies will be hard.

Shape dough into balls that are 1 inch in diameter. Flatten with a fork or spoon. Place on an ungreased cookie sheet and bake at 350 degrees F for 10 to 15 minutes, or until slightly browned on the bottom. Cool on a wire rack.

MAKES ABOUT 2½ DOZEN COOKIES

Krunch Bars

Krunch Bars

These bars are super easy and really good. Great for picnics or traveling as they don't crumble or fall apart.

⅔ cup butter, at room temperature
1 cup brown sugar
4 cups quick-cooking oats
½ cup light corn syrup

1 tablespoon vanilla
¾ cup chocolate chips
⅔ cup peanut butter

Preheat oven to 350 degrees F. Cream the butter and brown sugar together; add the oats, corn syrup, and vanilla. Spread into a greased 9 x 13-inch pan and bake for 15 minutes; let cool.

In top of a double boiler, melt the chocolate chips and peanut butter together; spread mixture evenly over the oatmeal mixture. When set, cut into squares or bars.

MAKES ABOUT 3 DOZEN BARS

Butterscotch Blondies

These wonderful bars are really like rich butterscotch brownies.

1½ cups butter, at room temperature
1½ cups brown sugar
2 eggs
1 tablespoon vanilla
2 cups unbleached flour

1½ teaspoons baking powder
½ teaspoon salt
¾ cup butterscotch morsels
¾ cup nuts (walnuts or pecans)

Preheat oven to 350 degrees F. In a large bowl, beat the butter and sugar together until smooth; beat in eggs and vanilla. In another bowl, combine the flour, baking powder, and salt; add to creamed mixture, blending well. Stir in the butterscotch morsels and nuts.

Spread batter evenly in a greased 9 x 13-inch pan. Bake for 20 to 25 minutes, or until a toothpick inserted in the center comes out clean. Let cool in pan on a wire rack and then cut into bars.

MAKES 12 TO 16 BARS

Cappuccino Coins

We blend the flavor of coffee and chocolate in these "little coins of caffeine bliss." These cookies are a favorite of Tassajara guests.

½ cup butter, at room temperature
½ cup sugar
½ cup dark brown sugar
4 eggs
4 cups unbleached flour
1 tablespoon instant coffee
1 tablespoon unsweetened cocoa powder
1 teaspoon cinnamon
½ teaspoon salt
1 cup semisweet chocolate chips, finely ground

Using an electric mixer, cream the butter and sugars together on medium speed until smooth. Scrape down the sides of the bowl with a rubber spatula and add eggs; mix well. Add the flour, instant coffee, cocoa, cinnamon, salt, and chocolate chips; mix thoroughly for 2 to 3 minutes.

Gather the dough together and turn onto a lightly floured board. Using lightly floured hands, roll the dough into 2 or 3 even 1-inch-thick logs. Wrap the logs separately in plastic wrap. Refrigerate until firm, about 1 hour.

Move oven rack to middle position. Preheat oven to 350 degrees F. Line a large cookie sheet with parchment paper. Slice the chilled logs into ¼-inch-thick coins and then place ½ inch apart on the lined cookie sheets.

Bake until the cookies are lightly golden and firm enough at the edges to slide off the parchment without sticking, about 15 to 17 minutes. Cool on the cookie sheets set on wire racks.

MAKES ABOUT 3½ DOZEN COOKIES

Orange-Pistachio Cookies

Orange and pistachio are a delicious flavor combination, and the pistachios add a delightful crunch to these soft cookies.

1½ cups butter, at room temperature
¾ cup sugar
2 eggs
½ teaspoon vanilla
½ teaspoon orange extract
3 cups unbleached flour
½ teaspoon salt
5 tablespoons orange zest
2 cups chopped pistachios (or toasted and skinned hazelnuts)

Preheat oven to 350 degrees F. Cream butter and sugar together; beat in eggs, vanilla, and orange extract.

In another bowl, combine flour, salt, and orange zest. Stir into butter mixture and then stir in nuts.

Roll dough into balls about 1 inch in diameter then flatten slightly with the back of a spoon. Place on a greased cookie sheet. Bake about 15 minutes, or until slightly brown around the edges. Cool on a wire rack.

MAKES ABOUT 3 DOZEN COOKIES

Tart Lemon Bars or Lemon Tart

These are buttery, sweet-tart dreams. The best of all lemon bar recipes combined to make The One. Serve these refreshing lemon bars or lemon tart as a finale for a special meal.

2⅓ cups unbleached flour, divided
1½ cups sugar, divided
2 teaspoons baking powder, divided
¼ teaspoon baking soda
½ teaspoon salt
1 cup butter, at room temperature
4 eggs
6 tablespoons fresh lemon juice
1½ teaspoons lemon zest

Preheat oven to 350 degrees F. To make the crust, mix together 2 cups flour, ½ cup sugar, 1 teaspoon baking powder, baking soda, and salt. Work in the butter to make a soft dough. Pat into a greased 9 x 13-inch pan and then bake for 20 minutes.

While the crust is baking, make the filling. Mix the remaining flour and baking powder and set aside. In another bowl, mix remaining sugar, eggs, lemon juice, and lemon zest. Stir in the baking powder mixture. Pour over the hot crust (it is important the crust be hot or the filling will not stick to it). Bake for 25 minutes, or until the filling is set.

VARIATIONS: *Pat crust into pie or tart tins and bake as tarts; glaze with sour cream. Roy from Israel doubled the sugar for the crust, and for the filling, he added orange extract and more lemon juice and lemon zest.*

MAKES ABOUT 3 DOZEN BARS

Mocha Shortbread Cookies

Use a good-quality chocolate to bring out the best in these rich butter cookies.

2 ounces bittersweet chocolate
2 cups unbleached flour
½ teaspoon baking powder
¼ teaspoon instant coffee
⅛ teaspoon cinnamon
1 cup butter, at room temperature
½ cup brown sugar
½ cup ground walnuts or almonds
walnuts or almonds, for garnish

Preheat oven to 350 degrees F. In the top of a double boiler, melt chocolate. Combine flour, baking powder, instant coffee, and cinnamon in a bowl and set aside.

In another bowl, cream the butter and sugar together; beat in the melted chocolate and ground nuts. Stir in the flour mixture.

Roll the dough into balls, about the size of a rounded tablespoon; flatten and then press in a walnut half or almond. Place on a greased cookie sheet and bake 10 to 15 minutes, but watch carefully as they are already brown. Cool on a wire rack.

MAKES ABOUT 3 DOZEN

VARIATION: *You can also reduce sugar slightly in recipe, and roll balls into sugar, then flatten and press with nuts.*

Dried Apricot Macaroons

These not too sweet gems are perfect for coconut lovers.

1 cup sugar
4 cups unsweetened flaked coconut, divided
1 cup chopped dried apricots
4 large egg whites
¼ teaspoon salt
1 tablespoon butter, melted
½ teaspoon almond extract
½ teaspoon vanilla

Preheat oven to 350 degrees F. Line cookie sheets with parchment paper. Mix sugar, 3 cups coconut, apricots, egg whites, and salt together with your hands. Add melted butter and extracts; combine well. Refrigerate for at least 1 hour.

Moisten the palms of your hands with cold water. Roll 1 tablespoon of the dough mixture between your palms, squeezing tightly together to form a compact ball. Roll each ball in remaining coconut.

Place on a greased cookie sheet about 1 inch apart. Bake until edges are golden brown, about 15 minutes. Cool on a wire rack.

MAKES 2 DOZEN COOKIES

VARIATION: *After forming dough into a compact ball, place on a clean surface and using a spatula, flatten one side at a time to form a pyramid shape. Bake as above and then let cool completely. Melt 3 ounces semisweet chocolate and 1 teaspoon butter in a bowl set over a pan of simmering water. Stir occasionally until melted. Dip top ½ inch of each pyramid into chocolate mixture.*

Nut-Chocolate Bars
"Unsurpassed"

These are a chewy and surprisingly moist cookie.

2 cups unbleached flour
1 teaspoon baking powder
¼ teaspoon baking soda
½ teaspoon salt
⅔ cup butter, at room temperature
2 cups brown sugar
2 eggs
2 teaspoons vanilla extract
2 cups chopped nuts
1½ cups chocolate chips

Preheat oven to 350 degrees F. In a medium bowl, combine the flour, baking powder, baking soda, and salt. Cream the butter and then add the sugar. While continuing to beat, add the eggs, vanilla, nuts, chocolate chips, and dry ingredients.

Spread in a greased 9 x 13-inch pan and bake for 30 minutes, or until done. While still warm, cut into squares or bars.

MAKES ABOUT 3 DOZEN BARS

Chewy Oatmeal Cookies
with Chocolate Chips and Coconut

Oatmeal cookies with chocolate chips and coconut—what could be better?

½ cup butter, at room temperature
½ cup brown sugar
½ cup white sugar
1 egg
½ teaspoon vanilla
¾ cup unbleached flour
½ teaspoon salt
½ teaspoon baking soda

½ teaspoon cinnamon
½ teaspoon cloves
½ teaspoon nutmeg
1½ cups quick-cooking oats
½ cup raisins
½ cup chocolate chips
¼ cup flaked coconut (optional)

Preheat oven to 375 degrees F. In a large bowl, cream butter and sugars together; beat in the egg and vanilla. In another bowl, mix the flour, salt, baking soda, cinnamon, cloves, nutmeg, and oats.

Gradually add the dry ingredients to the butter mixture, blending thoroughly. Stir in the raisins, chocolate chips, and coconut, if desired. Bake on an ungreased cookie sheet for 8 to 10 minutes. Cool on a wire rack.

MAKES ABOUT 2½ DOZEN COOKIES

Chocolate Truffles

Chocolate truffles couldn't be any easier. Try rolling the truffles in different coatings and leave some plain for a great visual effect. Chopped pistachios make a nice contrast to the dark chocolate.

1 pound semisweet chocolate (bittersweet bar or chocolate chips)
¾ cup heavy cream
½ cup unsweetened cocoa powder
chopped nuts and/or shredded coconut (optional)

Break or chop the chocolate into medium-sized pieces. Place it in the top of a small double boiler over hot water on low heat; cover and let stand until melted. Uncover and stir until completely melted and reaches 120 degrees F on a candy thermometer.

Remove the top of the double boiler and heat the cream to a boil; cool to 115 degrees F. Add the melted chocolate to the cream, stirring slowly until well combined. (If the chocolate cooled to lower than 115 degrees F, reheat to at least 115 degrees F.) Cover with plastic wrap and cool.

When the mixture is firm enough to hold a definite shape (like the consistency of peanut butter), place a piece of wax paper in front of you. Using a slightly rounded teaspoon or melon baller, scoop some of the mixture for each truffle. Roll each scoop into a ball and then roll in cocoa powder or chopped nuts and/or shredded coconut.

MAKES ABOUT 3 DOZEN COOKIES

Butterscotch-Chocolate Chip Brownies

Very quick brownies!

1½ cups butterscotch or chocolate chips or ¾ cup of both
½ cup butter, at room temperature
1 cup flour
4 eggs
1½ cups sugar
1 teaspoon vanilla
1 cup chopped cashews

Preheat oven to 350 degrees F. In a saucepan, melt the chocolate and/or butterscotch chips and butter over low heat. Remove from heat and beat in flour, eggs, sugar, and vanilla. Stir in cashews.

Pour into a greased 9-inch-square pan. Bake for 20 to 25 minutes, or until a toothpick inserted in the center comes out clean. Let cool in pan on a wire rack completely before cutting into bars.

MAKES ABOUT 1½ DOZEN BARS

$250 Neiman Marcus Cookies

Save these ultra rich cookies for a special occasion.

½ cup butter, at room temperature
½ cup white sugar
½ cup brown sugar
1 egg
½ teaspoon vanilla
1½ cups oatmeal, ground into a fine powder
¾ cup unbleached flour
¼ teaspoon salt
½ teaspoon baking powder
½ teaspoon baking soda
1½ cups semisweet chocolate chips
4 ounces Hershey's semisweet chocolate bar, grated
¾ cup chopped walnuts

Preheat oven to 375 degrees F. In a large bowl, beat the butter and sugars together until smooth and creamy. Beat in the egg and vanilla.

Combine the oatmeal, flour, salt, baking powder, and baking soda in a separate bowl and then add it to the creamed mixture and blend until smooth. Add the chocolate chips, grated chocolate bar, and walnuts; mix well.

Roll the dough into balls about 1 inch in diameter and place on lightly greased cookie sheet about 2 inches apart. Bake for 10 minutes. Cool on a wire rack.

MAKES ABOUT 2½ DOZEN COOKIES

vegan cookies & sweets

Date and Coconut Cookies
(Auntie Nuke's)

For the past twenty-five years, these vegan cookies have been requested by Tassajara guests.

½ cup nuts, roasted
½ cup date pieces
1½ teaspoons nutritional yeast
½ cup shredded coconut
2 cups unbleached flour*
½ teaspoon baking powder
¼ teaspoon salt
¾ cup maple syrup
1½ teaspoons vanilla
½ cup canola oil or other vegetable oil

Preheat oven to 325 degrees F. Put the nuts and date pieces into a food processor and chop together. Put mixture into a medium-sized bowl and then add the yeast, coconut, flour, baking powder, and salt; mix well.

In another small bowl, combine the maple syrup, vanilla, and oil. Mix into the dry mixture and stir together until the dough is firm and holds it shape. Spoon by tablespoon onto a greased baking sheet and bake for 20 to 25 minutes. Cool on a wire rack.

MAKES ABOUT 2½ DOZEN COOKIES

For a wheat-free alternative, blend baby oats until fine and use in place of flour.

Mixed Dream Cookies

These cookies are full of texture and just slightly sweet. Delicious with a fresh pot of tea.

½ cup dried apricots
1 cup mixed nuts, roasted (any combination such as walnuts, sunflower seeds, cashews, almonds, pumpkin seeds, peanuts)
½ cup soy margarine
¼ cup confectioners' sugar, sifted
1½ teaspoons vanilla
½ cup honey
1 cup unbleached flour
¼ teaspoon salt

Preheat oven to 325 degrees F. If the apricots seem very dry, soak in hot water and then drain, saving the liquid; chop apricots into small bits.

In a food processor, chop the mixed nuts; set aside. In a large mixing bowl, cream the margarine and then beat in the confectioners' sugar, vanilla, and honey.

In another bowl, combine the flour and salt; fold into the margarine mixture.

Add the nuts and chopped apricots and mix well. If the dough seems stiff, add some of the apricot soaking liquid. Use a small ice cream scoop or melon baller to drop dough onto greased baking sheets. Bake for 20 to 25 minutes, depending on the size of the balls. Cool on a wire rack.

MAKES ABOUT 1½ DOZEN COOKIES

Spicy Oatmeal Raisin Cookies

A traditional recipe adapted for vegan eating but with a unique blend of spices. Delicious!

3 cups rolled oats
1 cup unbleached flour
½ teaspoon salt
1 teaspoon baking soda
1 teaspoon cinnamon
1 teaspoon nutmeg
1 teaspoon ground ginger
1 teaspoon ground cumin
½ teaspoon black pepper

pinch of cardamom
pinch of cayenne pepper
1 banana, mashed
½ cup dry sweetener*
2 tablespoons oil
1 cup soy milk
1 teaspoon apple cider vinegar
¾ cup raisins
½ cup chocolate chips

Preheat oven to 375 degrees F. In a large bowl, stir the oats, flour, salt, baking soda, and spices together. Add the banana, sweetener, oil, soy milk, vinegar, raisins, and chocolate chips. Stir gently until just mixed.

Scoop tablespoon-sized portions onto a greased baking sheet and bake for 8 to 10 minutes for soft cookies, or 16 to 20 minutes for more crisp cookies. Cool on a wire rack.

Try using sucanat, sugar, or other alternatives. Some people choose to limit their intake of refined or simple sugar, here are some other alternatives to use in the cookies.

Sweetner	Substitute for each cup refined sugar	Reduced total liquid per cup of sugar
Barley malt or rice syrup	1½ cups	Slightly
Honey	¾ cup	⅛ cup
Fruit juice concentrate	¾ cup	⅛ cup
Maple syrup	¾ cup	⅛ cup
Molasses	½ cup	None

Lemon Poppy Seed Shortbread Cookies

These lemony cookies melt in your mouth.

2 cups unbleached flour
¼ cup poppy seeds
¼ cup arrowroot powder
½ teaspoon nutmeg
¼ teaspoon salt
1 cup margarine
⅔ cup dry sweetener*
3 tablespoons fresh lemon juice
2 tablespoons lemon zest
2 teaspoons vanilla

Preheat oven to 375 degrees F. Stir the flour, poppy seeds, arrowroot powder, nutmeg, and salt together. In another bowl, cream the margarine, sweetener, lemon juice, lemon zest, and vanilla.

Add the margarine mixture to the flour mixture and stir until just mixed. Using a tablespoon, spoon the dough onto a greased baking sheet. Bake for 10 to 12 minutes. Cool on a wire rack.

MAKES ABOUT 2½ DOZEN

VARIATION: *An alternative would be to roll out the dough ¼ inch thick, bake on a baking sheet, and then cut after baking*

*See page 187.

Lemon Cookies

Refreshingly light and tart, these lemon cookies are delicious!

½ cup rice or corn syrup
½ cup maple syrup
zest from 2 lemons
juice from 2 lemons
½ cup canola oil
1 cup unbleached flour
4 tablespoons arrowroot powder
¼ teaspoon salt

Preheat oven to 350 degrees F. Whisk the syrups, lemon zest, lemon juice, and canola oil together. In another bowl, combine flour, arrowroot powder, and salt.

Pour the syrup mixture into the flour mixture and whisk until combined. Spoon ½ table-spoons of dough onto baking sheets about 4 inches apart. Bake for 6 minutes and then rotate baking sheet, turn and bake other side; bake another 7 minutes, or until golden brown along the edges.

MAKES ABOUT 1½ DOZEN

VARIATION: *Press the dough balls flat after putting onto baking sheets.*

Non-Dairy Cocoa Cookies

Rich chocolate gems with just enough texture.

1 cup maple syrup
1 cup canola oil or other vegetable oil
1½ cups whole wheat pastry flour
½ cup rolled oats
½ cup cocoa powder
2 tablespoons arrowroot powder
½ cup chopped walnuts, almonds, or coconut

Preheat oven to 350 degrees F. Mix the syrup with the oil. In another bowl, sift the flour, oats, cocoa powder, and arrowroot. Stir in chopped nuts or coconut.

Pour the syrup mixture over the flour mixture and stir with as few strokes as possible so the dough is not over mixed. Drop by tablespoons onto a greased baking sheet about 1 inch apart. Bake for 15 to 18 minutes. The cookies will be soft and lightly brown at the bottom when done, do not over bake them. They will harden as they cool. Cool on a wire rack.

MAKES ABOUT 2½ DOZEN COOKIES

Pat Walton's Oatmeal Cookies

This recipe originated in the '70s at Tassajara. If carob doesn't appeal to you, you can substitute chocolate chips.

⅓ cup soy milk
½ teaspoon cider vinegar
½ cup margarine
¼ cup shortening
¾ cup brown sugar
½ cup honey
1½ teaspoons vanilla
¾ cup unbleached flour
½ teaspoon salt
½ teaspoon baking soda

¾ teaspoon cinnamon
½ teaspoon nutmeg
½ teaspoon cloves
¾ cup ground pecans
2 cups quick oats
½ cup raisins, soaked in water
¾ cup carob or chocolate chips
½ cup flaked coconut

Preheat oven to 350 degrees F. Combine the soy milk and cider vinegar and set aside in a warm place. Cream the margarine, shortening, brown sugar, honey, and vanilla together in a large bowl.

In another bowl, mix the flour, salt, baking soda, cinnamon, nutmeg, and cloves. Add to the margarine mixture along with the soy milk mixture; mix well. Stir in the pecans, oats, drained raisins, carob chips, and coconut.

Drop by tablespoon onto a greased baking sheet and bake for 12 minutes, or until done. Cool on a wire rack.

MAKES ABOUT 4 DOZEN (2½-INCH) COOKIES

Tim's Variation to Pat Walton's Oatmeal Cookies

Banana adds a creaminess and tropical flavor to these spicy oatmeal cookies.

½ teaspoon apple cider vinegar*
¼ cup soy milk*
1 banana, mashed
¼ cup canola oil
2 tablespoons molasses
¾ cup honey
¾ teaspoon vanilla
2½ cups baby rolled oats
1½ cups whole wheat flour, sifted

½ teaspoon salt
¾ teaspoon baking soda
1½ teaspoons cinnamon
¼ teaspoon nutmeg
¼ teaspoon cloves
1 cup pecans, chopped
1 cup chocolate chips
½ cup flaked coconut
pecan halves (optional)

Preheat the oven to 375 degrees F. Mix the cider vinegar and soy milk together and then set aside in a warm place until ready to use. Cream together the banana, oil, molasses, honey, vanilla, and oats.

In a separate bowl, combine the flour, salt, baking soda, cinnamon, nutmeg, and cloves. Add to the banana mixture and blend well. Mix in the pecans, chocolate chips, and coconut.

Drop by tablespoon onto a greased baking sheet. Press in a pecan half on top of cookie before baking if you like. Bake for 12 minutes. The cookies won't look done but they will firm up when cooled. Cool on a wire rack.

MAKES ABOUT 4 DOZEN COOKIES

*In place of apple cider vinegar and soy milk, you can use the "egg replacer" recipe below:

½ teaspoon soy flour
½ teaspoon arrowroot powder
pinch of lecithin
1½ teaspoons warm water

Thumbprints

One of the most popular vegan cookies. They are delicious, easy to make, and beautiful cookies. Also a great cookie to make with your children!

1 cup unbleached flour*
2 cups almonds, ground
4 cups baby rolled oats
½ teaspoon salt
1 cup maple syrup
1 cup canola oil or vegetable oil
½ cup jam, thinned with water

Preheat oven to 350 degrees F. In a medium-sized bowl, combine the flour, almonds, oats, and salt.

In another bowl, mix together the syrup and oil. Add to the dry ingredients using your hands and mix well. Let dough sit 15 minutes before using.

Roll dough into ¾-inch balls. Place close together on baking sheets. Make a little dent in the top of each ball and then fill with ½ teaspoon or less of the jam. Bake for 15 minutes, or until slightly brown. Do not over bake. Cool on a wire rack.

VARIATIONS: *Use honey in place of maple syrup, add ½ cup peanut butter and reduce oil by ¼ cup. Or use ½ cup honey and ½ cup maple syrup in place of 1 cup maple syrup and 1 cup mini chocolate chips.*

MAKES ABOUT 5 DOZEN

For wheat-free (no wheat flour), use finely blended baby oats.

No-Bake Cocoa-Coconut Sweets

These super easy cookies satisfy even the pickiest chocolate lover.

2½ tablespoons cocoa powder
¾ cup maple syrup
¼ cup soy milk
½ teaspoon vanilla
¼ cup margarine
1½ cups baby rolled oats
¼ cup peanut butter
1¾ cups flaked coconut, divided

Mix the cocoa and syrup together in a saucepan; add the soy milk, vanilla, and margarine; heat until liquefied and just reaches a boil. Stir the mixture, scraping the sides, being sure not to let it burn; cool mixture.

In a separate bowl, combine oats and peanut butter together using your hands. Next, pour in the cocoa mixture and add 1 cup coconut; blend with your hands until well mixed.

Roll dough into 1-inch balls. If the mixture is too wet, add more oatmeal or roll the balls into remaining coconut. They will be somewhat sticky but will harden as they cool. Put on a tray and store in refrigerator.

MAKES ABOUT 3 DOZEN COOKIES

Chocolate Chip Cookies

Orange extract brightens the flavor of these traditional chocolate chip cookies.

2½ cups whole wheat flour
1½ teaspoons baking powder
½ teaspoon salt
½ cup honey
½ cup maple syrup
⅓ cup canola oil or other vegetable oil
1 teaspoon orange extract
1 cup chocolate chips

Preheat oven to 350 degrees F. Sift flour, baking powder, and salt. In another bowl, mix honey and syrup together; stir in the oil. Add orange extract and beat until blended. Add flour mixture and mix well. If too wet, add more sifted flour.

Add chocolate chips and mix well. Drop by teaspoons on a greased baking sheet. Bake for 15 minutes, or until lightly browned. They will harden as they cool, be sure not to over bake. Cool on a wire rack.

MAKES ABOUT 2 DOZEN COOKIES

Chocolate-Peppermint Chocolate Chip Cookies

Not quite Girl Scout Thin Mints, but a delicious vegan alternative.

2¾ cups unbleached flour
½ cup cocoa
1½ teaspoons baking powder
½ teaspoon salt
½ cup margarine, softened or canola oil
1 cup maple syrup
1½ teaspoons peppermint extract
1 teaspoon vanilla extract
1½ cups chocolate chips

Preheat oven to 350 degrees F. Combine flour, cocoa, baking powder, and salt. In another bowl, beat the margarine, syrup, and peppermint and vanilla extracts together until smooth.

Add to the dry mixture and then stir in chocolate chips and mix. Drop by teaspoon onto a greased baking sheet; flatten with the back of a spoon. Bake 12 to 16 minutes. Cool on a wire rack.

MAKES ABOUT 2 DOZEN COOKIES

Siobhan's Granny's Matrimonial Cake (Date Bars)

A traditional date bar but made with margarine rather than butter.

1½ cups date pieces or pitted dates
½ cup warm water
2 cups flour
2 cups rolled oats
½ teaspoon salt
¾ cup maple syrup
½ cup margarine (or use ¾ cup vegetable oil and add another ½ cup flour)
1½ teaspoons vanilla

Preheat oven to 375 degrees F. Soften dates by soaking in warm water; then blend mixture in food processor until smooth and set aside. For the dough, mix flour, rolled oats, and salt. Combine syrup, margarine, and vanilla together; add to oat mixture. Spread the dough into a greased 9 x 13-inch pan as evenly as possible, reserving one-fourth for the topping. Next spread on reserved date mixture. Crumble reserved dough mixture over the date mixture. Bake for 30 to 35 minutes and then cool and cut into squares.

Note: If you use butter or margarine, cut it into the dry ingredients and then add ½ cup brown sugar. Save one-fourth for topping and reduce amount of maple syrup by ½ cup.

MAKES 12 TO 16 BARS

Maple-Coated Nuts

This recipe was first originated by Tassajara "old timer," Iva Jones. This became a bag lunch favorite that the Bag Lunch Crew tried to keep permanently stocked as people looked depressed when they were told them they weren't available that day. In peak season, a gallon of this recipe would only last about a week.

3 cups walnuts
salt, to taste
½ to ¾ cup maple syrup

Preheat oven to 350 degrees F. Line a baking sheet with wax paper. Fill pan with the walnuts in one layer; don't pile too much or the nuts won't roast well. Bake for 10 to 12 minutes.

Remove, and while still warm, put into a strainer and rub the walnuts against the side to remove the bitter skins. Put back onto pan and salt liberally to taste. Then pour enough maple syrup over the nuts so that they are thoroughly coated but not too gooey. Spread evenly into one layer with a spatula.

Return to oven for 10 to 15 minutes more, or until well-roasted. After removing from oven, stir well to eliminate sticking to the pan later.

MAKES 3 CUPS

Poached Spiced Figs

These delicious wine-soaked figs are a Bag Lunch favorite. Use fresh figs when available.

1½ cups fruity red wine
6 tablespoons sugar
1 x 3-inch-strip orange zest
6 peppercorns
1 whole clove
2 allspice berries
½ pound dried California figs

Bring all the ingredients but the figs to simmer in a non-corroding saucepan. Add the figs and cook them at a very slight simmer until they are tender when pierced with the tip of a knife. This will take anywhere from 30 minutes to 1½ hours, depending entirely on the figs.

Remove the figs to a container with a slotted spoon, raise the heat, bring the syrup to a boil, and reduce by one-third. Pour it over the figs and chill. They will keep for 1 to 2 weeks and will benefit from sitting in their syrup for a few days.

Serve with a little of their syrup and some cream to pour over top, or by themselves as a complement to a picnic, appetizer, or dessert.

MAKES ½ POUND

Peppered Mixed Nuts
with Lemon and Capers

This very popular nut mix served at the Bag Lunch at Tassajara is taken from Deborah Madison's book Vegetarian Cooking for Everyone. *Of course, it is adapted by whoever made it that day . . .*

1 cup capers
1½ cups canola oil
2 cups assorted roasted, unsalted nuts (about ½ pound)
2 teaspoons fresh lemon juice
½ teaspoon fresh-ground pepper, or to taste
2 teaspoons finely grated lemon zest

Preheat oven to 300 degrees F. Drain and rinse capers and then transfer to a paper towel–lined baking sheet; gently pat with more paper towels. Let dry completely for about 1 hour.

Heat oil in a medium saucepan until it registers 350 degrees F on a deep-fry thermometer. Carefully add ¼ cup capers and fry, stirring constantly, until golden brown, about 3 minutes. Using a long-handled slotted spoon, transfer capers to a paper towel–lined baking sheet. Adjusting the heat as necessary to maintain oil temperature, continue adding capers in ¼ cup increments until all the capers have been fried. Reserve 2 tablespoons of the cooking oil; let cool.

In a bowl, toss nuts with reserved oil, lemon juice, and pepper. Spread mixture evenly on a rimmed sheet pan. Toast nuts in oven, stirring occasionally, until golden brown, about 25 minutes. Remove from oven; let cool, about 20 minutes. Sprinkle with lemon zest and then toss with fried capers. Mixture can be stored in an airtight container at room temperature up to 2 weeks.

MAKES 2 CUPS

Mixed Nut Granola
with Oat Bran

Granola used in the Bag Lunch at Tassajara is meant to be a sweet snack. It can be combined with dried fruits and nuts as part of a trail mix or as a topping for yogurt. This recipe can even be eaten by itself as a rich, concentrated source of protein and carbohydrates.

⅓ cup sunflower, soy, or canola oil
¼ cup maple syrup
3 tablespoons honey
1½ teaspoons vanilla extract
⅛ teaspoon almond extract
¾ teaspoon cinnamon
⅛ teaspoon ground allspice
½ teaspoon salt
½ cup flaked wheat
½ cup oat bran
2½ cups rolled oats
½ cup raw cashews, chopped
½ cup raw almonds, chopped
½ cup raw pecans, chopped

Preheat oven to 350 degrees F. Mix oil, syrup, honey, extracts, cinnamon, allspice, and salt in a bowl.

In a separate large bowl, mix the remaining ingredients together. Toss the oil mixture with the dry ingredients and mix to coat thoroughly. Spread the mixture on two sheet pans and bake until golden brown, about 30 minutes. Stir after 15 minutes so that it browns evenly. Cool completely and then store in a tightly covered jar.

MAKES ABOUT 5 CUPS

Almond-Sunflower Seed Granola

This recipe for a more "traditional" granola. It has more oats and less nuts and even less sweetener, so it's a bit lighter than Mixed Nut Granola with Oat Bran (see page 205).

4 cups rolled oats
⅓ cup raw wheat germ
⅓ cup almonds
⅓ cup sunflower seeds
1½ teaspoons cinnamon
¼ teaspoon nutmeg
¼ teaspoon salt
⅓ cup raisins
¼ cup canola oil
¼ cup maple syrup
1 teaspoon vanilla extract
⅛ teaspoon almond extract

Preheat oven to 350 degrees F. Mix rolled oats, wheat germ, almonds, sunflower seeds, cinnamon, nutmeg, salt, and raisins in a large bowl.

In a separate bowl, combine the oil, syrup, and extracts and then add to dry ingredients. Mix thoroughly until well coated. Spread the mixture on two sheet pans and bake until golden, for about 30 minutes. Stir after 15 minutes so that it browns evenly. Cool completely and then store in a tightly covered jar.

MAKES ABOUT 5 CUPS

"Ritual, prayer, your innermost request—please find your own way to bring yourself to your meal, to sitting down at the table and taking the time to eat with gratitude, enjoyment, and gusto."

—EDWARD ESPE BROWN

Composing Your
Moveable Feast

"Take the time to give each task its due—it comes out in the food: a generosity of spirit. Call it rejoicing, tenderness, graciousness, or simple attention to detail, the quality of caring is an ingredient everyone can taste."

—TENZO KYOKUN (INSTRUCTIONS FOR THE TENZO)

There are many ways to create a sandwich as there are sandwiches. Be adventurous and see for yourself.

Making a Sandwich

"Spreads are used to make sandwiches more interesting." —Edward Brown

One way to make a sandwich is to put any spread, pâté, or sandwich filling on a slice of bread, add some fresh-sliced or roasted vegetables, and spread mayonnaise, chutney, or aioli on the other slice of bread to finish things off.

Sonja, the Tenzo at Tassajara, says to start with a protein base (cheese or tofu), add some roasted or raw vegetables in the middle, and put a different spread on each slice of bread. She also recommends using rolled up lettuce instead of bread to hold the sandwich fillings. Edward Brown sometimes puts five spreads on both bread slices so that every bite has a different taste.

If you are trying to cut down on bread products or wheat, there are many alternatives to bread included in the following pages. Try using the various suggestions and more.

In terms of condiments, try Rosemary Aioli, Cashew Butter, or even chutneys to make your sandwiches more exciting. Chutneys add a special zest to sandwiches—whether heating them up or cooling them down.

Homemade pickled vegetables, marinated artichokes, green olives, and other tart, pickled things are good served alongside your sandwich.

Nuts accent meals with their rich flavor and texture. Nutritionally they are excellent sources of the "good fats," protein, vitamins and minerals, and a small amount goes a long way. At Tassajara, we offer granola as a sweet treat or as an alternative to cookies or trail mix. It offers the sweetness of cookies and trail mix, but is much lighter.

Try a whole new taste with these combinations of spreads, pâtés, and chutneys:
Honey Mustard Tofu with Pineapple Chutney
Roasted Vegetables with Marinated Tofu and Rosemary Aioli
Leek Cream Cheese with Sweet Vegetable Tapenade
Herb-Crusted Tofu with Basil "Cream" and Pickled Red Onions

Accoutrements

These are some of the offerings at the Tassajara Bag Lunch. Include as many as you like in your lunch or picnic.

CONDIMENTS:

Stone-ground mustard
Yellow mustard
Mayonnaise
Nayonnaise
Herb-infused olives
Olive oil
Red wine vinegar
Peanut butter
Jelly

PICKLES/OLIVES:

Green olives
Kalamata olives
Nicoise olives
Pickled cucumbers
Mini pickles
Marinated mushrooms
Capers
Pepperocini
Marinated potatoes

CHEESES/BUTTERS/EGGS:

Swiss cheese
Gouda cheese
Monterey Jack cheese
Vermont cheddar cheese
Plain cream cheese
Feta cheese
Red pepper cream cheese
Chipotle cream cheese
Garlic butter
Chipotle butter
Deviled eggs

Hard-boiled eggs

VEGETABLES:

Lettuce
Sliced tomatoes
Cherry tomatoes
Heirloom tomatoes
Sliced cucumbers
Avocado halves
Carrot sticks
Celery sticks
Radishes
Jicama
Raw cauliflower
Raw broccoli
Raw red, green, and yellow bell peppers
Sliced onions
Alfalfa sprouts
Pea sprouts
Fresh herbs-parsley, tarragon, oregano, dill
Roasted shitake mushrooms
Roasted fennel
Roasted zucchini
Roasted garlic
Roasted mushrooms with fresh herbs
Roasted bell peppers
Roasted eggplant

OTHER:

Fresh fruit
Lemon wedges
Dried fruit
Granola

Where Do I Put My Spreads?

Use the items below instead of bread to serve alongside spreads, pâtés, and vegetables for a picnic, or as a base for appetizers.

INSTEAD OF BREAD
(RECIPES BELOW)

Crostini
Crispy tortilla cups
Crunchy flour tortilla triangles
Bruschetta
Stuffed zucchini cups
Wonton wedges
Bagel chips
Croustades
Pita crisps
Filo cups

OTHER IDEAS:

Crisp potato slices
Cucumber slices
Stuffed hard-boiled rggs
Hollowed-out/stuffed red/green peppers, tomatoes, and other vegetables

Hollowed-out fruits
Toasted party rye
Crispy breadsticks
"On leaves"-Romaine, endive, radicchio…
Lebanese pita bread (thicker pita bread with no pocket)
Lavosh (for pinwheels)
Puff pastry
Pumpernickel bread
Mini toasts
Melba toast
Spring roll wrappers
Rice paper wrappers
Wonton skins
Flour or corn tortillas or "wraps" (for pinwheels)
Crackers: Ak Mak, water, rye krisp, rice
Rice cakes

CROSTINI

These are crusty Italian toasts.

Preheat the oven to 400 degrees F. Cut a baguette into ⅓-inch-thick slices. Lightly brush both sides with olive oil. Arrange the slices in a single layer on a baking sheet and bake for 2 minutes on each side, or until golden brown. They will harden as they cool. Serve at room temperature.

TOAST POINTS

Try, wheat, rye, or even pumpernickel bread.

Trim crusts off sandwich bread, then cut each slice in half on the diagonal. Or use a cookie cutter to cut into other shapes such as hearts, stars, etc. Arrange the bread on a baking sheet in a single layer and bake at 350 degrees F for 5 minutes on each side, or until dry and lightly toasted. The toast points can also be grilled for 3 to 5 minutes.

CRISPY TORTILLA CUPS

Try flavored tortillas or wraps to add color and flavor.

Preheat oven to 350 degrees F. Using a knife or biscuit cutter, cut flour or corn tortillas into 4-inch rounds. Make four equally placed ½-inch cuts around the edge of the tortilla. Wrap the tortillas in foil and heat in the oven for 5 minutes, or until soft. Cover to keep warm. Place the tortillas into lightly oiled muffin cups, overlapping where the cuts meet. Lightly brush with olive oil and bake for 10 to 12 minutes, or until crispy. They will firm up as they cool. Let cool on a wire rack.

CRUNCHY FLOUR TORTILLA TRIANGLES

An alternative to corn chips.

Preheat the broiler. Cut 8-inch tortillas into fourths (or more, if you want smaller pieces); brush both sides lightly with olive oil. Place on a baking sheet and prick the surface in several places with a fork. Broil 4 to 5 inches from the heat for about 1 to 2 minutes on each side, or until lightly browned. Watch carefully as they toast quickly. Put on a plate to cool. They will get crunchier as they cool.

BRUSCHETTA

These are small, toasted bread slices.

Slice fresh or day-old French or Italian bread into ½ to ¾-inch-thick slices. Preheat the broiler, a stovetop grill to 400 degrees F, or a toaster oven. Toast or grill the bread in one layer, until both sides are golden brown and crisp on the outside, yet still chewy on the inside. If using an oven, bake for about 3 minutes on each side. If using a broiler, the time will be less so watch to prevent the bread from burning.

STUFFED ZUCCHINI CUPS

These tiny cups are attractive and a nice way to add more vegetables to your diet.

Using two 8-inch zucchini, trim and discard the ends of both. Cut the zucchini crosswise into ¾-inch-thick slices. Using a melon baler, scoop out the center of each slice, leaving a shell a little less than ¼ inch thick. Steam the cups in a covered steamer until just barely tender, about 4 minutes. Drain the cups upside down on a plate covered with a paper towel.

WONTON WEDGES

For added flavor, sprinkle lightly with Parmesan cheese or dried herbs such as oregano, basil, or thyme.

Preheat oven to 375 degrees F. Lightly brush a baking sheet with butter. Cut a stack of wonton skins in half diagonally. Place the triangles in a single layer on the baking sheet and brush the tops lightly with butter. Bake for 4 to 5 minutes, or until golden brown. Remove from baking sheet and cool on a wire rack.

BAGEL CHIPS

Use a variety of bagels for added flavor and color. Day-old bagels work great!

Preheat oven to 375 degrees F. Cut each bagel into six ¼-inch-thick rounds. Cut in half again for half moon shapes or break the toasted rounds into smaller chips after cooling. Place the slices in a single layer on a baking sheet. Toast the slices in the oven for 6 to 8 minutes, turning once, or until lightly browned on both sides and crisp.

CROUSTADES

Try these tasty and tiny toasted bread cups.

Preheat the oven to 350 degrees F. Cut fresh wheat, white, or other type of bread, into 3-inch rounds. Gently press into mini-muffin cups and bake for about 10 minutes, or until the bread cups are lightly browned. Let cool in the pan on a wire rack.

PITA CRISPS

These crisps are best when prepared just before using. For added flavor, sprinkle with Parmesan cheese and dried oregano or basil.

Split horizontally one 6- or 7-inch white or whole wheat pita round. Preheat the broiler.

Arrange the pita halves, rough-side up, on a baking sheet. Lightly brush with olive oil. Using kitchen shears, cut each pita half into 8 triangles. Broil for about 2 minutes, or until the triangles are lightly browned and the cheese is melted, if using. Be careful to watch closely so they don't burn. Serve warm or at room temperature.

FILO CUPS

A light and delicate way to present rich fillings.

Thaw 4 sheets frozen filo dough. Preheat oven to 350 degrees F. Place 1 filo sheet on a cutting board and lightly brush with melted butter. Top with the remaining sheets, stacking one at a time and lightly brushing each layer with butter. Cut the stacked sheets into 12 squares. Mold the squares into muffin cups, allowing the pointed ends to extend above the cups. Bake for 4 to 6 minutes, or until golden brown. Let cool in pans on a wire rack.

Lunch Bag Ideas

I've included this section to present environment-friendly ways to pack your lunch or picnic. No need to throw anything into the landfill with these wonderful storage containers. Food also stays fresh and either hot or cold eliminating the need to microwave or refrigerate!

LUNCH BAGS	STORE	PRICE $
Super Lunch Bag	LL Bean	15.00
Nylon Lunch Totes and Sacks	The Container Store	4.99–12.99
Deluxe Lunch Bag with Cooler	PriceHot.com	6.99
Deluxe Insulated Picnic Cooler	PriceHot.com	9.99
PLASTIC STORAGE CONTAINERS		
Lunch on the Go	Chef's Catalog	14.99
Lunch N 'Things Container	Tupperware	11.00
Insulated Containers, snack jars	Home Village Wholesale	2.99–9.99
Heavy Duty		
Thermal Lunch Box and Caddy	Home Village Wholesale	9.99
Laptop Lunch System	American Style Bento Boxes and Lunch Jars	11.99–19.99
The Lunch Date	Laptop Lunches	33.99–124.99
STAINLESS STEEL CONTAINERS		
Stainless Thermos Lunch Jars	Tiger, Nissan	11.99–45.99
3 Tier Chinese Lunch Box	The Wok Shop	24.95
"Ms. Bento" Stainless Lunch Jar comes with cloth bag	iKitchen.com	39.99
Nissan Wide Mouth Thermos Lunch Tote TLN 1400x	Zaccardi's	36.95
Bombay Express "Lunch Box"	Asiana West	12.95
555 Stainless Lunch Box	Asiana West	12.95–14.95
Bento-Hakoya Collection Japanese Lunch Box	Asiana West	24.95
Executive Mini Vacuum Thermos with strainer and infuser	Asiana West	29.95–30.95
Japanese Lunch Jars	Zojirushi	53.99
Wide Stainless Thermos	The Gourmet Kitchen	36.99

Index

Metric Conversion Chart

Liquid and Dry Measures

U.S.	Canadian	Australian
¼ teaspoon	1 mL	1 ml
½ teaspoon	2 mL	2 ml
1 teaspoon	5 mL	5 ml
1 Tablespoon	15 mL	20 ml
¼ cup	50 mL	60 ml
⅓ cup	75 mL	80 ml
½ cup	125 mL	125 ml
⅔ cup	150 mL	170 ml
¾ cup	175 mL	190 ml
1 cup	250 mL	250 ml
1 quart	1 liter	1 litre

Temperature Conversion Chart

Fahrenheit	Celsius
250	120
275	140
300	150
325	160
350	180
375	190
400	200
425	220
450	230
475	240
500	260